PREFACE

Thank you for choosing to teach your students the English language with this textbook. Obtaining fluency in  libly difficult endeavor, even when the langua spread use across the globe like English. I my e for nearly twenty years during my time as a translator in Kyoto, and although I consider myself fairly proficient, I know that there is still much more for me to learn, as well as much that I will never master. But that's okay. The process has been enjoyable, thanks in large part to wonderful instructors and textbooks. Likewise, I hope this textbook can serve as a tool for you, the teacher, to provide your students with fun and engaging lessons in a subject that, quite frankly, can be a challenging one in terms of motivating students.

They say you should write what you know, and so again, as I did with "America Today: Culture, Society and History," I am writing about my home country, the United States of America. Working with my excellent editor, Keiko Nagano, we have come up with chapters containing a variety of topics so that any student will find something of interest, whether it be popular culture, social issues, or something a little offbeat like the origin of the doggie bag or unusual local laws. (I personally think South Carolina's age limit on playing pinball is the most surprising.)

Each chapter contains a reading passage and several exercises to build vocabulary, practice reading comprehension, and construct sentences with proper grammar. I also encourage you to be creative in how you use the contents to teach your classes, according to the level of your students. To get your students to practice producing original English on their own, I recommend organizing a discussion activity for each chapter. However you decide to design your lessons, I hope you and your students have a lot of fun.

Lastly, I would like to thank my editor Keiko Nagano for all her hard work, especially for sharing her perspective and great ideas for topics that really rounded out the chapters. And of course, thank you to everybody at the publisher, Shohakusha, who was involved in producing this textbook. I look forward to collaborating on many more projects in the future.

Alexander Farrell

America's Evolution

CONTENTS

Unit 1
Customs
America's Biggest
Family Holiday
3

Unit 2
Culture
The Hawaiian Language
and
Identity Today
8

Unit 3
Society
Who's an Adult
in America?
13

Unit 4
Entertainment
When Does a Joke
Cross the Line?
18

Unit 5
Customs
Doggie Bags
for Humans?
23

Unit 6
Economics
The Almighty Dollar
28

Unit 7
Nature
The Mt. St. Helens
Eruption
33

Unit 8
Education
The Cost of College
38

Unit 9
Film
The Legacy of
The Godfather
43

Unit 10
Identity
Transgender Athletes
48

Unit 11
Literature
A Poem for a President
53

Unit 12
Sport
Who Were the Washington
Redskins and
the Cleveland
Indians?
58

Unit 13
Society
Weird Laws
63

Unit 14
Work
Careers in Crisis
68

Unit 15
Politics
What Is *Roe v. Wade*?
73

各章のリーディング本文は 2023 年 2 月時点での情報をもとにしています。

UNIT 1

Customs

America's Biggest Family Holiday

★★★ ─────────────

文化が異なれば、祝日の習慣もそれぞれに異なります。日本では、お正月やお盆に多くの家族が集まりますが、アメリカにはお正月やお盆の習慣はありません。しかし、アメリカにも家族と過ごす祝日があります。その中でも、家族で過ごす最大の祝日は何の日だと思いますか？
さっそく本章を読んでみましょう。

───────────── ★★★

≡≡≡ **Pre-reading Section** ≡≡≡

Vocabulary — Fill in the Blank

日本語訳をヒントに、空所に入る最も適切なものを次の中から選び、書き入れなさい。ただし、文により形を変える必要があるものが含まれています。

| with a bang | gunfire | heavily | kick off | else | certain |

1. 気候変動を止めるには、二酸化炭素の排出を大幅に削減しなければならない。

We have to ＿＿＿＿ reduce carbon emissions if we're going to stop climate change.

2. 試合は開始 1 分でホームチームがゴールを決め、華々しく始まった。

The game began ＿＿＿＿ when the home team scored a goal in the opening minute.

3. 自分の妹を信じられないなら、あなたは他に誰を頼りにできるのですか？

If you can't trust your own sister, who _____ can you rely on?

4. 一攫千金を狙うにはそれなりの運が必要だ。

Your plan to get rich quick will require a _____ amount of luck.

5. もし銃声が聞こえたら、すぐに隠れてください。

If you hear _____, take cover immediately.

Reading

346 words   🔊 Audio 02

❶ Can you name an American holiday? You're probably thinking of Christmas. But did you know the biggest family occasion in America is Thanksgiving, on the fourth Thursday of November? That's why the days before and after are the busiest and most expensive time to travel
5 in the U.S. Thousands of Americans living overseas also flock home to visit relatives for Thanksgiving.

❷ What do Americans do on this holiday? Each family has its own traditions, but many Americans stay at home for the day snacking, watching holiday programming or football games on TV, or playing their
10 own family football game outside in the yard, until the big feast[*1] at dinnertime. Traditional dishes include turkey, stuffing,[*2] mashed potatoes, and cranberries, with pumpkin pie for dessert. The main reason most people stay home on Thanksgiving is that there's usually not much else to do since almost all local businesses are closed.

15 ❸ But stores reopen with a bang the next day. This is Black Friday, when retailers typically put on huge sales to kick off the holiday shopping season that runs until Christmas. Black Friday has gained a certain amount of notoriety[*3] for chaotic scenes of crazed shoppers tearing into stores the second they open, racing to get their hands on a
20 limited number of heavily discounted big-ticket items like TVs. The name Black Friday supposedly comes from the idea that this season is

when many retailers make enough sales to go into the black (i.e., turn a profit) for the year.

❹ As for the origins of Thanksgiving, it dates back to colonial New England.*4 Thanksgivings to celebrate successful harvests were common affairs among English settlers back then, but the traditional story of the 5 first such feast is about a friendly celebration between the Pilgrims, a group of English settlers, and a local Native American tribe in 1621. During a Pilgrim harvest feast, celebratory gunfire caused concern among the nearby Wampanoag tribe, but when they investigated and discovered the festivities, they were relieved. The Pilgrims welcomed the 10 tribesmen and together they socialized and shared food and drink for several days.

---

*1 **feast** ごちそう
*2 **stuffing** 詰め物。家庭によって様々な種類のレシピがあるが、フランスパンやバゲットのような硬めのパンを刻んで、玉ねぎ、セロリ、バター、卵、肉または野菜からとった出汁、ハーブ（パセリやローズマリーなど）を混ぜて焼く。
*3 **notoriety** 悪評、不評
*4 **New England** 13 植民地のうち北東部のコネチカット、ロードアイランド、メイン、マサチューセッツ、ニューハンプシャー、バーモントの 6 州を指す。正式に「州」になったのは、1776 年の独立宣言とその後のアメリカ独立戦争を経たあとのことである。

≡ Post-reading Section ≡

Vocabulary　Fill in the Blank

日本語訳をヒントに、空所に入る最も適切なものを次の中から選び、書き入れなさい。ただし、文により形を変える必要があるものが含まれています。

investigate　　turn a profit　　tear　　snack　　run　　flock

1. 夏休みの間じゅう、家族連れが海辺に集まります。
During summer vacation, families _____ to the beach.

2. このような競争の激しい業界で利益を出すのはとても難しい。
It's so hard to _____ in a competitive industry like this.

3. 家の中を散らかすのをやめないなら、デザートはないからね！

No dessert for you if you don't stop _____ through the house!

4. 彼女は政府のために保険金詐欺の事例を調査している。

She _____ cases of insurance fraud for the government.

5. ほとんどのテレビ番組は、数シーズン以上放送されることはありません。

Most TV shows don't _____ for more than a few seasons.

Vocabulary ╲ Synonym Practice

英英・英日の語義が成立する単語になるよう、頭文字をヒントに空所を埋めなさい。もしわからないときは、本文中から適切な単語を探して埋めましょう。

1. event = o *ccasion*　出来事、大事な行事

2. a _ _ _ _ _ = situation, matter　事態

3. beginnings, start = o _ _ _ _ _ _ _　はじまり

4. s _ _ _ _ _ _ = some, more than a few　いくつかの

5. p _ _ _ _ _ _ _ _ _ _ = TV shows　番組

6. disorderly, frenzied = c _ _ _ _ _ _ _　大混乱の

7. n _ _ _ _ _ _ _ _ = infamy, a bad reputation　悪評

8. overly excited, wild = c _ _ _ _ _ _　熱狂的な

9. r _ _ = last　続く

10. s _ _ _ _ _ _ _ _ _ = apparently, reportedly　おそらく

Comprehension Questions ╲ True or False

本文の内容として正しい場合は T、間違っている場合は F を書き入れなさい。

1. Black Friday sales run until Christmas.

2. Most Americans eat Thanksgiving dinner at a restaurant.

3. The story of the first Thanksgiving involved English settlers and Native Americans.

1. (　　　) 2. (　　　) 3. (　　　)

Comprehension Questions **Multiple Choice**

本文の内容について最も正しく述べているものを a ～ c の中から選びなさい。

1. What does "the yard" in the second paragraph of the reading passage mean?
   a. any yard in the neighborhood
   b. the yard on the family's property
   c. the yard that everyone in the neighborhood shares

2. According to the passage, what is so exciting about Black Friday sales?
   a. big discounts on everyday items
   b. big discounts on imported items
   c. big discounts on expensive items

3. What does "the first such feast" in the final paragraph of the reading passage mean?
   a. the first Thanksgiving
   b. the first Black Friday
   c. the first football game

Composition with Typical Expressions   Audio 03

よく使われる英語の表現を学習しましょう。日本語訳を参考に、（　　）内の単語を正しい語順に並び替えて文にしなさい。

1. その限定シューズはどうやって手に入れたのですか？

   (did, limited-edition, how, get, hands, those, on, you, shoes, your)?

   _____

2. 今年は黒字にするのは不可能だ。

   (black, impossible, to, go, it's, the, year, this, into).

   _____

3. 空港に着いたらすぐに電話してね。

   (second, airport, call, the, the, arrive, me, at, you).

   _____

UNIT

2

Culture

The Hawaiian Language and Identity Today

★★★

ハワイ旅行を計画している人は現地で使える英語表現を勉強しているかもしれませんが、ハワイ諸島の一部の人々によって先祖代々の言語で州の公用語でもあるハワイ語が今も使われていることを知っていますか？ハワイ語は絶滅しかけていたために実現が困難だった言語復活の試みなのです。

─────────── ★★★

Pre-reading Section

Vocabulary   Fill in the Blank

日本語訳をヒントに、空所に入る最も適切なものを次の中から選び、書き入れなさい。ただし、文により形を変える必要があるものが含まれています。

| immersion | translation | resident | official | standard | territory |

1. 日本の公用語は 1 つだけです。それは日本語です。

Japan has only one _____ language: Japanese.

2. アメリカのある州の住民であれば、その州の公立大学の授業料が安くなります。

If you're a _____ of a U.S. state, your tuition at that state's public colleges is lower.

3. 私は社員に高水準のカスタマーサービスを期待している。

I expect a high _____ of customer service from my employees.

4. 語学は集中訓練なら楽しく学べるが、文法をきちんと勉強するのを忘れてはいけない。

_____ can be a fun way to learn a language, but don't forget to properly study the grammar.

5. グアムはアメリカの領土であり、州ではない。

Guam is a U.S. _____ , not a state.

Reading

347 words　Audio 04

❶ Hawaiian is the indigenous language of the Hawaiian Islands, but only 0.1% of the state's residents speak it today. Originally, it was a spoken language, but it also became a written one in the 19th century when Christian missionaries used the Roman alphabet to provide Hawaiian translations of the Bible. ⁵

❷ Hawaiian has similarities with Japanese. In Hawaiian, all words end in a vowel,[*1] a vowel must follow every consonant,[*2] every syllable[*3] ends with a vowel, and two consonants can never follow one another. Written Hawaiian has 13 letters: A, E, I, O, U, H, K, L, M, N, P, W, and '. The vowels are pronounced the same way Japanese people pronounce them. ¹⁰ The last letter, represented by an apostrophe, separates vowels with a glottal stop,[*4] or slight pause. That's why sometimes you may see Hawai'i instead of Hawaii.

❸ After the United States overthrew the Hawaiian Kingdom in 1893 and made the islands a U.S. territory in 1898, the indigenous language ¹⁵ was banned in schools and government, though people still used it in conversation and local newspapers. Over time, Hawaiian fell into widespread disuse, one reason being the educational and career advantages English offered throughout the U.S. This pattern of a dominant language[*5] pushing out a minor one has been repeated ²⁰

★★★

throughout history.

❹ Modern communications have accelerated the trend. Certain languages are becoming standard for business, government, and cultural works over increasingly larger geographical areas. A dominant language can also
5 affect identity. As each generation uses it more, their connection with the indigenous culture weakens.

❺ That connection, however, has not disappeared in Hawaii. Nearly two decades after Hawaii became the 50th U.S. state in 1958, Hawaiian's revival took a major step forward when it was recognized as an official
10 language of the state in 1978, alongside English. There are also Hawaiian language immersion schools. Another interesting thing: While a New Yorker, for example, can be anyone who was born in or currently lives in New York, a Hawaiian is only a person of ethnic Hawaiian descent, while other people living in the state are called Hawaii residents.

---

*1 **vowel** 母音
*2 **consonant** 子音
*3 **syllable** 音節
*4 **glottal stop** 声門閉鎖音（「えっ！」と驚いて発声したときなど、声門の一時的な閉鎖またはその開放によって出る音）
*5 **dominant language** 主要な言語

≡ **Post-reading Section** ≡

Vocabulary　Fill in the Blank

日本語訳をヒントに、空所に入る最も適切なものを次の中から選び、書き入れなさい。ただし、文により形を変える必要があるものが含まれています。

| descend | revive | recognize | affect | represent | overthrow |

1. 選手の負傷がこの試合の結果を左右するかもしれません。
Player injuries could _____ the outcome of this game.

2. 私は自国を代表してオリンピックに参加したことをとても誇りに思う。
I am so proud to have _____ my country at the Olympics.

★★★

3. アイヌ語は日本の公用語として認められていない。

Ainu is not _____ as an official language of Japan.

4. 外国の諜報員がわが国の政府の転覆を企んでいる！

Foreign spies are plotting to _____ our government!

5. 伝統的な祭りを復活させることは、私たちの小さな町にこそ必要なことなのかもしれない。

_____ the traditional festival could be just what our small town needs.

Vocabulary　Synonym Practice

英英・英日の語義が成立する単語になるよう、頭文字をヒントに空所を埋めなさい。もしわからないときは、本文中から適切な単語を探して埋めましょう。

1. d _ _ _ _ _ _ _ _ = major, main　主要な

2. popular, common = w _ _ _ _ _ _ _ _ _ _　普及した

3. i _ _ _ _ _ _ _ _ _ = local, native　先住の

4. benefits = a _ _ _ _ _ _ _ _ _　利点

5. t _ _ _ _ _ _ _ _ _ = everywhere, in its entirety　至るところに

6. c _ _ _ _ _ _ _ _ = presently, now　現在のところ

7. a _ _ _ _ _ _ _ _ _ _ = sped up, made faster　加速された

8. b _ _ _ _ _ = prohibited　禁じられた

9. more and more = i _ _ _ _ _ _ _ _ _ _ _ _　ますます

10. a _ _ _ _ _ _ _ _ _ = next to, with　～と並行して、～とともに

Comprehension Questions　True or False

本文の内容として正しい場合は T、間違っている場合は F を書き入れなさい。

1. Every syllable in Hawaiian must contain a consonant.

2. The Hawaiian language used to be banned in schools and government.

3. A Hawaiian is not a person who moved to Hawaii from another state.

1. (　　　) 2. (　　　) 3. (　　　)

Comprehension Questions   Multiple Choice

本文の内容について最も正しく述べているものを a 〜 c の中から選びなさい。

1. What is a glottal stop?
   a. a slight pause between letters in a written text
   b. a slight pause between letters in a spoken language
   c. a slight pause between sentences in a conversation

2. How did Hawaiian become a written language?
   a. Christian missionaries interpreted the Bible into Hawaiian
   b. Christian missionaries wrote a new Bible for the Hawaiians
   c. Christian missionaries translated the Bible into Hawaiian

3. How does a dominant language affect identity?
   a. it spreads over a wider geographical area
   b. it weakens the connection with the indigenous culture
   c. it strengthens the connection with the indigenous culture

Composition with Typical Expressions   Audio 05

よく使われる英語の表現を学習しましょう。日本語訳を参考に、（　　）内の単語を正しい語順に並び替えて文にしなさい。

1. デザインコンテストでの受賞は、私のファッションデザイナーとしての大きな一歩となりました。

   (design contest, major step, fashion designer, winning a, was a, career, in my, forward).

   _____

2. 外国産の魚が湖の固有種を駆逐してしまった。

   (pushed out, a foreign, indigenous species, species of fish, has, the lake's).

   _____

3. ラテン語はヨーロッパで支配的な言語であったが、次第に使われなくなった。

   (Europe, Latin, gradually, fell into, was a, disuse, dominant, in, language, that).

   _____

★ ★ ★

12

UNIT
3
Who's an Adult in America?

Society

★ ★ ★

2022 年 4 月 1 日より日本の成人年齢が 20 歳から 18 歳に引き下げられました。米国では、18 歳からが法的に成人とされて久しいですが、18 歳になったからといって何でも許されるわけではありません。

一方で、米国では 18 歳になる前に成人としての恩恵を受けられることがいくつかあるようです。

—————————— ★ ★ ★

═══ **Pre-reading Section** ═══

Vocabulary　**Fill in the Blank**

日本語訳をヒントに、空所に入る最も適切なものを次の中から選び、書き入れなさい。ただし、文により形を変える必要があるものが含まれています。

| legal | shall | serve | define | substance | constitution |

1. 日本国憲法は米国がほとんどの部分をつくったって知っていましたか？

Did you know that America mostly wrote Japan's ＿＿＿＿＿ ?

2. ここでお酒を飲むなら身分証明書がないといけません。

You have to have a valid I.D. to be ＿＿＿＿＿ alcohol here.

3. 税関職員が彼女が所持していた薬を規制薬物だと思ったので、彼女は逮捕された。

She was arrested because the customs officials thought her medicine was a controlled _____ .

4. 浮気？！　それが浮気の定義なの？　僕は電話で彼女にアドバイスをしただけなのに！

Cheating?! That's how you _____ cheating? All I did was give her some advice on the phone!

5. この規則を破った者は一週間の居残りをさせられる。

Anyone caught breaking this rule _____ be given one week of detention.

Reading

346 words　🔊 Audio 06

❶ It's hard to define exactly when an adolescent becomes an adult. Is it when your body undergoes certain biological*¹ changes? When you're financially independent? When you're old enough to legally enjoy mind-altering*² substances like alcohol and cigarettes or, in some states,
5 marijuana?

❷ The United States has minimum age requirements for a variety of activities that have evolved*³ over the years. When these laws change, it is often in response to shifting public opinion. A good example is the 26th Amendment to the U.S. Constitution, ratified in 1971. This simple
10 amendment states, "The right of citizens of the United States, who are eighteen years of age or older, to vote shall not be denied or abridged by the United States or by any State on account of age." Until then, each state determined its own voting age. Most set it at 21. However, men only had to be 18 to join the military or be drafted. Around this time,
15 thousands of young American men had been dying in the Vietnam War. A growing segment of the American population found it hypocritical*⁴ to allow them to go fight and die for their country, but not have the right to choose the leaders who send them into battle.

❸ The 1970s was also when the minimum legal drinking age was at its
20 lowest in most states, ranging between 18 and 21. Today, however, you must be 21 to purchase alcohol anywhere in the U.S. Interestingly, the

★ ★ ★

minimum age to serve alcohol at a restaurant or bar is 18 in many states and only 17 in Maine. As for cigarettes, 18-year-olds could purchase them until December 2019, when the minimum age was raised to 21. It's also 21 for marijuana...in states that have legalized the drug.

❹ So if you're 18, what can you do besides vote and join the army? Buy a ₅ gun. And you only need to be 16 to get a driver's license. What about working a part-time job? A 14-year-old can do that. It was also possible to get married in Alaska at that age until March 2022.

*1 **biological** 生物学的に
*2 **mind-altering** 精神に変化をきたす
*3 **evolve** 考案する、発展する
*4 **hypocritical** 偽善的な

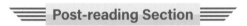

=== **Post-reading Section** ===

Vocabulary   Fill in the Blank

日本語訳をヒントに、空所に入る最も適切なものを次の中から選び、書き入れなさい。ただし、文により形を変える必要があるものが含まれています。

> undergo   ratify   deny   legalize   draft   range

1. 上司がまったく合理的な休暇申請を認めなかったなんて信じられない！

I can't believe my boss _____ my completely reasonable vacation request!

2. 日本は第二次世界大戦後、徴兵制を採用していない。

Japan hasn't _____ soldiers for its military since World War II.

3. 憲法改正を法律として成立させるには、州の４分の３が批准する必要がある。

An amendment to the Constitution must be _____ by three-fourths of the states to become law.

4. 手術を受けるのは不安だ。

I'm nervous about _____ surgery.

5. 日本で野球賭博がすぐに合法化されるとはとても思えない。

I seriously doubt betting on baseball will be _____ in Japan anytime soon.

Vocabulary | Synonym Practice

英英・英日の語義が成立する単語になるよう、頭文字をヒントに空所を埋めなさい。もしわからないときは、本文中から適切な単語を探して埋めましょう。

1. a _ _ _ _ _ _ _ _ _ = young person （思春期の）若者

2. h _ _ _ _ _ _ _ _ _ _ _ = insincere, phony　偽善的な、でっちあげの

3. other than = b _ _ _ _ _ _　～のほかに

4. a _ _ _ _ _ _ _ _ = revision, change　修正

5. s _ _ _ _ _ _ = section, part, portion　部分

6. declare, say = s _ _ _ _　述べる、宣言する

7. a _ _ _ _ _ _ = shorten, reduce　短縮する

8. doable, could happen = p _ _ _ _ _ _ _　可能性がある

9. d _ _ _ _ _ _ _ _ = decide, control　決定する

10. g _ _ _ _ _ _ = increasing, enlarging　増える、高まる

Comprehension Questions | True or False

本文の内容として正しい場合は T、間違っている場合は F を書き入れなさい。

1. You can get married in Alaska at age 14.

2. The 26th Amendment allows each state to set its own voting age.

3. Marijuana is legal in some states.

1. (　　　) 2. (　　　) 3. (　　　)

Comprehension Questions　Multiple Choice

本文の内容について最も正しく述べているものを a ～ c の中から選びなさい。

1. When does an adolescent become an adult?
   a. the passage doesn't say
   b. after certain biological changes
   c. when you can vote

2. What was one major reason why the voting age was reduced from 21 to 18?
   a. because you could drink alcohol at age 18
   b. because young men were dying in Vietnam
   c. because you can buy a gun at age 18

3. What can you do if you're 18 years old?
   a. vote, buy alcohol, and get married in Alaska
   b. vote, buy cigarettes, and buy a gun
   c. vote, buy a gun, and serve alcohol in many states

Composition with Typical Expressions　🔊 Audio 07

よく使われる英語の表現を学習しましょう。日本語訳を参考に、（　　）内の単語を正しい語順に並び替えて文にしなさい。

1. この世代のキャリアアップの機会は、経済的に自立することを困難にする。

   (generation's, independent, this, make, hard, be, career, to, opportunities, financially, it).

   _____

2. 富士山に登ると心が洗われるような体験ができる。

   (can, Mt., experience, be, a, Fuji, climbing, mind-altering).

   _____

3. 彼は素行が悪いという理由で退学させられた。

   (kicked, behavior, he, his, account, school, of, on, out, bad, was, of).

   _____

UNIT 4

When Does a Joke Cross the Line?

Entertainment

★★★

米国のコメディアンの多くは、たとえ人を不快にさせるジョークであっても、自分にはどんなジョークも言う権利があるのだと頑なに主張します。しかし、観客の中には、あるジョークで非常に気分を害したとき、コメディアン側の主張を受け入れがたい人がいるかもしれません。そのような不快感にはどのように対処するのが正しいのでしょうか。

★★★

©PictureLux／アフロ

俳優・コメディアンのデイヴ・シャペル。『デイヴ・シャペルのこれでお開き（原題: *The Closer*)』（2021、Netflix）でのジョークを巡り、配信元の Netflix 社員や LGBTQ₈ コミュニティから猛烈な反発やバッシングを受ける騒動が起きた。

===== Pre-reading Section =====

Vocabulary　Fill in the Blank

日本語訳をヒントに、空所に入る最も適切なものを次の中から選び、書き入れなさい。ただし、文により形を変える必要があるものが含まれています。

| potential | offend | unjustified | criticize | cancel | stand up |

1. 彼が私の髪をからかったとき、どうして味方になってくれなかったの？

Why didn't you _____ for me when he was making fun of my hair?

2. 私の音楽が気に障るなら、聴かないでください。

If my music _____ you, then don't listen to it.

3. 侵略は完全に不当な暴力行為である。

The invasion is a completely _____ act of violence.

4. 私の上司は決して建設的なフィードバックを与えない。彼女は私の仕事を批判するだけだ。

My boss never gives me constructive feedback. She just _____ my work.

5. 彼女の勇気ある行動は、私たちの命を救う可能性がある。

Her act of bravery has _____ saved our lives.

Reading

349 words　🔊 Audio 08

❶ On March 27, 2022, comedian Chris Rock was hosting the 94th Academy Awards, also known as the Oscars. In the audience were Will Smith and his wife, Jada. She had been shaving her head because she had alopecia,[*1] a medical condition that causes partial hair loss. Rock ad-libbed a joke comparing Jada Smith to the main character in the movie 5 *G.I. Jane*, who in the film shaves her head. Will Smith initially laughed, but his wife seemed annoyed. Then, moments later, Smith walked onto the stage and slapped Rock on live television. The audience was stunned. At first, some thought it was part of a comedic act. Smith then shouted to Rock not to talk about his wife, using an expletive as he did so. Later, 10 Smith apologized directly to Rock and publicly, describing his behavior as "shocking, painful, and inexcusable." Smith also resigned as a member of the Academy of Motion Picture Arts and Sciences, the body that organizes the Oscars.

❷ The big question is: Did Chris Rock's joke cross the line?　15

❸ Public opinion polls showed that most Americans supported Rock and thought that Will Smith's use of violence was unjustified. Some described the slap as an act of toxic masculinity,[*2] which refers to traditional ideas of manhood that encourage and praise men for employing aggressive behavior and asserting their social dominance. A 20 typical example of this increasingly out-of-date[*3] attitude[*4] is the saying "boys will be boys," which adults may use to excuse bullying and fighting among adolescent males.

❹ Supporters of both Rock and Smith have also described the incident as an example of cancel culture. This is a phrase that refers to ostracism,[*5]
5 either online or face-to-face, in response to a person—usually a celebrity—who has done or said something that offends the ostracizing group. Some commentators have described Smith's behavior as cancel culture because of his strong reaction to speech he found offensive. Others have criticized Smith's fall from grace as canceling by his critics that has potentially
10 ruined the career of a celebrity who was standing up for his wife.
❺ What do you think?

---

*1 **alopecia** 脱毛症
*2 **toxic masculinity** 有害な男らしさの概念、男性性
*3 **out-of-date** 時代遅れの、古くさい
*4 **attitude** ふるまい、態度
*5 **ostracism** 社会的な追放

Post-reading Section

Vocabulary　Fill in the Blank

日本語訳をヒントに、空所に入る最も適切なものを次の中から選び、書き入れなさい。ただし、文により形を変える必要があるものが含まれています。

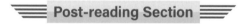

stun	employ	ostracize	assert	ad-lib	resign

1. 彼女はストレスに対処するためにユーモアを取り入れている。

   She _____ humor to deal with her stress.

2. 会議ではもっと自己主張しないと、誰もあなたの話を聞いてくれませんよ。

   If you don't _____ yourself more in meetings, nobody will listen to you.

3. もしこの仕事がこんなに大変だと知っていたら、私はもっと早く辞めていただろう。

   I would have _____ sooner if I'd known this job was going to be so tough.

4. 僕はセリフのリハーサルは必要ないんだ。どうせアドリブでやるつもりだから。

I don't need to rehearse my lines. I plan to just _____ anyway.

5. 首都でのテロ攻撃は国中を驚かせた。

The terrorist attack in the capital has _____ the nation.

Vocabulary   Synonym Practice

英英・英日の語義が成立する単語になるよう、頭文字をヒントに空所を埋めなさい。もしわからないときは、本文中から適切な単語を探して埋めましょう。

1. p _ _ _ _ _ _ = some, not all 部分的に

2. e _ _ _ _ _ _ _ _ = swear word, curse word, bad word, foul language 罵り言葉

3. manliness = m _ _ _ _ _ _ _ _ _ _ 男らしさ

4. p _ _ _ _ _ _ _ _ _ _ = possibly 可能性がある

5. c _ _ _ _ _ _ _ _ = famous person 有名人

6. irritated, bothered = a _ _ _ _ _ _ いらいらした

7. r _ _ _ = destroy 台無しにする

8. common expression, adage, proverb = s _ _ _ _ _ ことわざ、格言

9. in the beginning = i _ _ _ _ _ _ _ _ 最初は

10. i _ _ _ _ _ _ _ _ _ _ = intolerable 許し難い

Comprehension Questions   True or False

本文の内容として正しい場合は T、間違っている場合は F を書き入れなさい。

1. Will Smith slapped Chris Rock as a joke.

2. Chris Rock organized the Oscars.

3. The phrase "cancel culture" refers to a form of ostracism.

1. (   ) 2. (   ) 3. (   )

Comprehension Questions Multiple Choice

本文の内容について最も正しく述べているものを a 〜 c の中から選びなさい。

1. Why did Will Smith slap Chris Rock?
   a. Chris Rock shaved Jada Smith's head
   b. Chris Rock made a joke about Jada Smith's hair loss
   c. Chris Rock slapped Will Smith's wife

2. What did polls indicate about Americans' opinions about the incident?
   a. most thought Will Smith's behavior was wrong
   b. most thought Will Smith's behavior was justified
   c. most thought Will Smith's behavior was not violent

3. Which of the following is an example of what some people call "cancel culture"?
   a. a customer canceling an order for a pizza delivery at the last minute
   b. an airline canceling your flight after you've already arrived at the airport
   c. social media users spamming a celebrity's account with comments criticizing their opinion

Composition with Typical Expressions Audio 09

よく使われる英語の表現を学習しましょう。日本語訳を参考に、(　　)内の単語を正しい語順に並び替えて文にしなさい。

1. そのスキャンダルにより、社長は一気に失脚した。
   (president, the, swift, fall, scandal, the, a, grace, from, resulted, for, in).

   _____

2. 私は男の子は男の子らしくという古風な考えを受け入れることができません。
   (accept, boys, can't, the, that, boys, I, will, idea, old-fashioned, be).

   _____

3. 私にとってはあの広告の性差別は、一線を越えている。
   (sexism, ad, crosses, line, the, the, me, for, that, in).

   _____

UNIT

5

Customs

Doggie Bags for Humans?

★★★

新型コロナウイルスの大流行で恩恵を受けたビジネスの一つとして、自宅で楽しめる食事の宅配（フードデリバリー）があげられます。では、外食したとき食べ残した物を自宅に持ち帰るのはどうでしょうか。日本では衛生上の理由により浸透していませんが、アメリカではごく一般的で、その食べ残しを入れる容器を「ドギーバッグ」と呼んでいます。

★★★

Pre-reading Section

Vocabulary　Fill in the Blank

日本語訳をヒントに、空所に入る最も適切なものを次の中から選び、書き入れなさい。ただし、文により形を変える必要があるものが含まれています。

| appetite | uneaten | despite | short supply | practice | eats |

1. おなかがすいたよ。角の店でおいしいものを食べよう。

I'm starving. Let's get some yummy _____ at the corner store.

2. ロシアがウクライナに侵攻して穀物が不足した。

Grain went into _____ after Russia invaded Ukraine.

3. アメフトを始めた息子は食欲旺盛になった。

My son has a much bigger _____ after he started playing football.

★★★

23

4. チップはアメリカのレストランでは一般的だが、時に複雑な慣習だ。

Tipping is a common but sometimes complex _____ at American restaurants.

5. 私たちのチームはとても勝ち目がないにもかかわらず、試合に勝った。

Our team won the game _____ very long odds.

Reading

343 words 🔊 Audio 10

❶ As you may know, Americans have a reputation for consuming lots of food. And not just at home. Restaurants typically serve much larger meals than in most other countries. In fact, despite many Americans' voracious appetites, often even they are unable to clean their plate at a
5 restaurant. That's when it's time to request a doggie bag.

❷ Wait, what do canines have to do with uneaten food? According to dictionary publisher Merriam-Webster,[*1] a doggie bag (or doggy bag) is "a container for leftover food to be carried home from a meal eaten at a restaurant." But that doesn't answer our question. To figure it out, we have
10 to go back to World War II. At the time, one way Americans dealt with food shortages[*2] was to give leftovers[*3] from home-cooked meals to their pets. Restaurants later got in on the act by offering takeout boxes so customers could feed[*4] uneaten portions to their animal companions, which were in many cases dogs. Some diners then began asking for "doggie bags" to save
15 food for themselves, not their pets. Perhaps they didn't own any, or maybe they just didn't feel like giving them such good eats.

❸ Traditionalists frowned upon doggie bags as a crude practice, but some restaurants added a sophisticated touch by shaping the tin foil[*5] covering the leftovers into decorative designs like swans or seahorses.[*6]
20 Doggie bags designed specifically to carry bottles of wine gave the containers even more cachet. However, there are still upscale restaurants that look down on the use of doggie bags, not just the tacky name.

★★★

❹ Today, environmentally conscious diners have found further justification to ask for a doggie bag: food loss. Although food has not been in short supply in the U.S. over the decades since World War II, these restaurant-goers think they can reduce the environmental impact of farming and ranching by avoiding needless waste. And if you feel hesitant 5 to ask for a "doggie bag" even though you want to save the planet, remember that there are plenty of alternatives like "to-go box" or "takeout container."

---

*1 **Merriam-Webster** メリアム・ウェブスター社（アメリカ最古の辞書出版社）
*2 **food shortage** 食糧不足
*3 **leftover** 食べ残し、料理の余り物
*4 **feed** 食べさせる、与える
*5 **tin foil** アルミホイル
*6 **seahorse** タツノオトシゴ

≡ Post-reading Section ≡

Vocabulary　Fill in the Blank

日本語訳をヒントに、空所に入る最も適切なものを次の中から選び、書き入れなさい。ただし、文により形を変える必要があるものが含まれています。

deal　look down　avoid

consume　reduce　feel like

1. お寿司を食べたくなかったのなら、どうして注文する前にそう言わなかったの？

If you didn't _____ eating sushi, then why didn't you say so before we ordered?

2. パンダは一日あたり約 20 キロの竹を頻繁に食べるそうですよ。

I read that pandas often _____ around 20 kilograms of bamboo a day.

3. 彼女は夫の飲酒問題に対処することに疲れたため離婚してしまった。

She got a divorce because she's tired of _____ with her husband's drinking problem.

4. 貧しいからといって人を見下すようなことをしてはいけません。

You shouldn't _____ on someone just because they're poor.

5. もしこの通りで渋滞が起きると知っていたら、そこを避けていたのになあ。

If I'd known there'd be a traffic jam on this street, I would have _____ it.

Vocabulary ◦Synonym Practice

英英・英日の語義が成立する単語になるよう、頭文字をヒントに空所を埋めなさい。もしわからないときは、本文中から適切な単語を探して埋めましょう。

1. c _ _ _ _ = unsophisticated　雑な、こなれていない

2. t _ _ _ _ = in poor taste　趣味が悪い、ダサい

3. fancy = u _ _ _ _ _ _　高級な

4. status, prestige = c _ _ _ _ _　名声

5. uncertain, tentative = h _ _ _ _ _ _ _ _　消極的な

6. v _ _ _ _ _ _ _ _ = insatiable, extremely hungry　貪欲な

7. n _ _ _ _ _ _ _ = unnecessary, pointless　無用の、不必要な

8. aware = c _ _ _ _ _ _ _ _　意識している

9. a _ _ _ _ _ _ _ _ _ _ = option, another possibility　ほかの可能性、選択肢

10. c _ _ _ _ _ = dog　犬、イヌ科の動物

Comprehension Questions True or False

本文の内容として正しい場合は T、間違っている場合は F を書き入れなさい。

1. There is no alternate spelling for "doggie bag."

2. Food was in short supply in America during World War II.

3. There is more than one way to ask for a doggie bag.

1. (　　　) 2. (　　　) 3. (　　　)

★★★

Comprehension Questions Multiple Choice

本文の内容について最も正しく述べているものを a ～ c の中から選びなさい。

1. Which answer best describes why Americans started using doggie bags at restaurants?

   a. so they could eat more food

   b. so they could feed their pets

   c. so they could own more pets

2. How did restaurants try to make doggie bags more sophisticated?

   a. by adding free bottles of wine to the containers

   b. by frowning

   c. by making decorative designs with tin foil coverings

3. According to the passage, what is a reason why environmentally conscious diners may use doggie bags?

   a. to reduce food loss

   b. to needlessly waste

   c. to look cool

Composition with Typical Expressions 🔊 Audio 11

よく使われる英語の表現を学習しましょう。日本語訳を参考に、（　　）内の単語を正しい語順に並び替えて文にしなさい。

1. お皿を片付けても、デザートしか出てきませんよ。

   (plate, dessert, you, clean, if, you, get, only, your).

   _____

2. 僕の父さんもアカウントを作って TikTok を楽しむようになったんだ。

   (TikTok, get in, made, dad, account, the act, to, on, a, my).

   _____

3. たいていの上司は、職場でビデオゲームで遊ぶことに眉をひそめる。

   (upon, games, most, video, frown, work, playing, at, bosses).

   _____

The Almighty Dollar

★★★

金の威力 (Almighty dollar) ということばを聞いたことがありますか？ 米ドルには、他の国 (それはたとえ日本のような豊かな国であっても) にはないある種の強みがあります。しかし、一枚の紙幣と他の紙幣とでは何が違うのでしょうか。少しだけ込み入った話になりますが、本章で勉強してみましょう。

★★★

Pre-reading Section

Vocabulary　Fill in the Blank

日本語訳をヒントに、空所に入る最も適切なものを次の中から選び、書き入れなさい。ただし、文により形を変える必要があるものが含まれています。

| sanction | relative | combatant | dispute | currency | inflation |

1. 日本では過去数十年間、インフレ率は一般的に低い。

　　_____ has typically been low in Japan for the past few decades.

2. 日本では自動販売機を見つけるのは比較的簡単である。

　　It's _____ easy to find a vending machine in Japan.

3. 彼女は元夫との争いを法廷で解決しなければならないかもしれない。

　　She may have to settle her _____ with her ex-husband in court.

4. 北朝鮮に対する制裁は、この孤立した共産主義国に変化をもたらすのにほとんど役立っていない。

_____ against North Korea have done little to effect change in the isolated communist country.

5. なぜドルが世界通貨で円でないのか不思議だ。

I wonder why the dollar is the global _____ and not the yen.

Reading

343 words 🔊 Audio 12

❶ Most governments issue their own currency so citizens can buy and sell goods and services. Americans use the dollar and the Japanese use the yen. But there are many foreign countries where American tourists can spend with their dollars. Not so many for the yen. What makes the dollar so special? Why do people want to use it more than other ⁵ currencies?

❷ The complex answer begins over a century ago. By the time World War I broke out in 1914, the United States had already surpassed Great Britain as the world's largest economy. During the war, some governments started paying for their expensive armies with paper ¹⁰ money instead of gold, leading to serious inflation. World War II was even more expensive. And as in the previous conflict, the U.S. did not join the hostilities[*1] in the beginning. To fund their military campaigns, some combatants paid the U.S. in gold to obtain weapons and supplies. After the war, the U.S. was the largest holder of gold. This made it ¹⁵ impossible for borrowing countries to use the gold standard to determine the value of their currencies, as had been commonplace before. Therefore, the U.S. and 44 other countries agreed[*2] to peg their currencies to the U.S. dollar. Instead of building up reserves of gold, they accumulated dollars. ²⁰

❸ Although most exchange rates now float rather than being pegged, the dollar remains the world's reserve currency. This demand for dollars

★★★

and its relative stability in the eyes of governments, banks, and investors[3] means it is essential for international commerce. Since everyone uses dollars, they are a simpler medium of exchange,[4] even if none of the parties to a transaction are based in the U.S. This is why, for
5 example, oil is mostly traded in dollars.

❹ This demand for dollars means American economic sanctions against countries with which the U.S. government has a dispute,[5] such as Iran, North Korea, and more recently Russia, can have such a crippling impact. And that is one reason why the "almighty dollar" is so powerful.
10 But will it always be that way?

---

*1 **hostilities** （複数形で）戦争行為
*2 **the U.S. and 44 other countries agreed** 1944 年にニューハンプシャー州のブレトンウッズで開催された連合国国際通貨金融会議。このときに締結した協定により、米ドルを基軸に各国の通貨の為替相場を一定に保つことによって経済を安定させる仕組みをつくった（ブレトン＝ウッズ体制）。
*3 **investor** 投資家
*4 **medium of exchange** 貨幣、通貨
*5 **dispute** 異議を唱える

≡ Post-reading Section ≡

Vocabulary ⟍ Fill in the Blank ⟍

日本語訳をヒントに、空所に入る最も適切なものを次の中から選び、書き入れなさい。ただし、文により形を変える必要があるものが含まれています。

| issue | float | trade | peg | borrow | lead to |

1. 私が発行した新しい暗号通貨を買いたいですか？

Do you want to buy the new cryptocurrency I've _____ ?

2. 香港ドルは米ドルに (為替レートが) 連動している。

The Hong Kong dollar is _____ to the U.S. dollar.

3. COVID-19 により、国境を越えた取引はかなり難しくなった。

COVID-19 made it much more difficult to _____ across borders.

★★★

4. 通貨が変動する場合、政府が固定為替レートを維持しないことを意味する。

If a currency _____ , that means the government doesn't keep it at a fixed exchange rate.

5. もしあなたが銀行からお金を借りたら、それは銀行があなたに資金を貸すことを意味します。

If you _____ money from the bank, that means the bank will lend you funds.

Vocabulary　Synonym Practice

英英・英日の語義が成立する単語になるよう、頭文字をヒントに空所を埋めなさい。もしわからないときは、本文中から適切な単語を探して埋めましょう。

1. r _ _ _ _ _ _ _ _ = backup, extra amount　準備金、予備

2. ordinary, routine = c _ _ _ _ _ _ _ _ _ _　ありふれた

3. c _ _ _ _ _ _ _ _ = painful, very damaging　壊滅的な打撃を与える

4. c _ _ _ _ _ _ = complicated, not simple　複雑な

5. s _ _ _ _ _ _ = exceed　〜を超過する、しのぐ

6. c _ _ _ _ _ _ _ = fighting　争い

7. deal, exchange = t _ _ _ _ _ _ _ _ _ _　取引、経済活動

8. o _ _ _ _ _ = get　獲得する

9. decide, control = d _ _ _ _ _ _ _ _　決定する

10. a _ _ _ _ _ _ _ _ _ = collect, gather, build up　集める

Comprehension Questions　True or False

本文の内容として正しい場合は T、間違っている場合は F を書き入れなさい。

1. The U.S. obtained a lot of gold during World War II.

2. The gold standard allowed currencies to float.

3. Oil is traded in yen.

1. (　　　) 2. (　　　) 3. (　　　)

Comprehension Questions   Multiple Choice

本文の内容について最も正しく述べているものを a 〜 c の中から選びなさい。

1. Why did many countries drop the gold standard after World War II?
   a. because some had bought too much gold from the U.S.
   b. because some hadn't joined the hostilities in the beginning
   c. because some had used too much of their gold to buy weapons and supplies from the U.S.

2. What was one effect of pegging currency exchange rates to the U.S. dollar?
   a. countries reduced their reserves of dollars
   b. countries increased their reserves of dollars
   c. countries didn't change their reserves of dollars

3. Why do American economic sanctions have such a strong impact?
   a. because the dollar is used for a large amount of international commerce
   b. because the dollar is used for a small amount of international commerce
   c. because the dollar is used for no international commerce

Composition with Typical Expressions   🔊 Audio 13

よく使われる英語の表現を学習しましょう。日本語訳を参考に、（　）内の単語を正しい語順に並び替えて文にしなさい。

1. 夏は屋外でマスクをする人があまりいない。
   (people, many, not, masks, outside, so, in, wear, summer).

   _____

2. 蓼食う虫も好き好き（美は見つめる人の中にある）。
   (in, beholder, the, is, eyes, beauty, of, the).

   _____

3. 当社はその契約の当事者です。
   (party, our, to, agreement, company, is, a, the).

   _____

UNIT 7

Nature

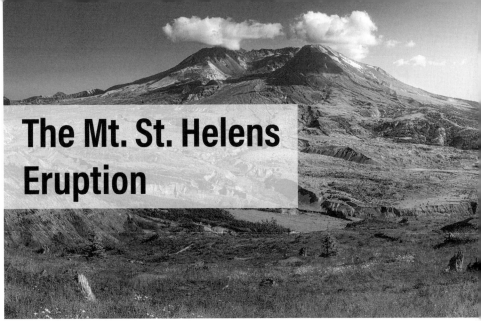

The Mt. St. Helens Eruption

©Gareth Janzen / Shutterstock.com

★★★

日本は地震や台風などの自然災害が多い国として知られていますが、米国にも自然災害がかなりあります。中でも、過去数十年で最も破壊的な災害の一つが、1980年に起きたワシントン州にあるセント・ヘレンズ山の噴火でした。

─────────────────────── ★★★

═══ **Pre-reading Section** ═══

Vocabulary ╲ Fill in the Blank

日本語訳をヒントに、空所に入る最も適切なものを次の中から選び、書き入れなさい。ただし、文により形を変える必要があるものが含まれています。

| seismic | elevation | plume | aquatic | cataclysm | nutrient |

1. 彼女は水生生物が好きなので、海洋生物学者になりたいそうです。

   She wants to become a marine biologist because she loves _____ life.

2. 日本は世界で最も地震が多い国の一つです。

   Japan is one of the world's most _____ active countries in the world.

3. 富士山の大噴火は、周辺地域に地殻変動をもたらすだろう。

   A major eruption of Mt. Fuji would be a _____ for the surrounding area.

4. 標高が高くなると空気が薄くなる。

   The air gets thinner at a high _____ .

5. 作物にもっと栄養を与えないと十分に育たないだろう。

   Our crops won't grow enough unless we give them more _____ .

❶ Americans can ski in the mountains, sunbathe on the beach, or ride horses across wide open plains without ever leaving their country. But diverse geography[*1] also creates various natural disasters. There are earthquakes and massive forest fires on the West Coast, tornadoes
5 screaming across the Great Plains, hurricanes battering[*2] the Gulf Coast, and blizzards buffeting the Northeast.

❷ There are also volcanoes. On May 18, 1980, the most destructive volcanic eruption[*3] in American history occurred at Mt. St. Helens. At the time, scientists were monitoring seismic activity there because minor
10 eruptions a couple months earlier had attracted their attention. They caught the sudden, enormous eruption on film, giving Americans a dramatic and detailed look at the disaster as it unfolded.

❸ Before the eruption, Mt. St. Helens had an elevation of 9,677 feet.[*4] In addition to a plume of volcanic ash that darkened the sky hundreds of
15 miles away, an earthquake caused a colossal landslide. After the disaster, the mountain's elevation had fallen to 8,363 feet. The landslide[*5] and tremendous[*6] heat melted and even boiled centuries-old glaciers.[*7] The resulting flood caught local residents unawares. Fortunately, because the area was sparsely populated, only 57 people
20 died, but so did thousands of animals and trees. In the decades since, there has been sporadic seismic activity and some small eruptions.

❹ Today, the area is designated Mt. St. Helens National Volcanic Monument. Geologists study the active volcano's mechanisms and biologists research how ecosystems respond to cataclysms. There is plenty of life around the volcano now. The volcanic ash provided nutrients to aquatic life that helped their populations grow rapidly, 5 while new plants and animals have recolonized the blast zone on land.

❺ There are also many people. The monument is open to tourists, who can view the horseshoe-shaped crater from an observatory*8 less than five miles away. Hikers traverse the slopes year-round. However, a word of caution: Scientists predict that future eruptions will be more 10 destructive because the current lava dome*9 will require greater pressure to burst than it did in 1980.

---

*1 **geography** 地形
*2 **batter** 打ちのめす
*3 **eruption** 火山の噴火
*4 **9,677 feet** 約2,950m（1フィート＝30.48cm）
*5 **landslide** 地滑り
*6 **tremendous** とてつもない、凄まじい
*7 **glacier** 氷河
*8 **observatory** 展望台
*9 **lava dome** 溶岩ドーム

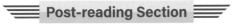

Post-reading Section

Vocabulary　Fill in the Blank

日本語訳をヒントに、空所に入る最も適切なものを次の中から選び、書き入れなさい。ただし、文により形を変える必要があるものが含まれています。

| respond | darken | designate | unfold | provide | predict |

1. この写真は、シャドウ（影になっている部分）を暗くすればもっときれいになります。

This photo will look nicer if we can _____ the shadows.

2. このレポートは、地震がどのように発生したかを詳しく分析している。

This report _____ a detailed analysis of how the earthquake occurred.

3. 株式市場がどうなるかを予測することは不可能だ。

It's impossible to _____ what the stock market will do.

4. 市長はこの家を歴史的建造物に指定するでしょう。

The mayor will _____ the house as a historic building.

5. ラグビーの試合が展開されるにつれて、訪問チームが簡単に勝つとだんだん明らかになってきた。

As the rugby match _____ , it gradually became clear that the visiting team would win easily.

Vocabulary Synonym Practice

英英・英日の語義が成立する単語になるよう、頭文字をヒントに空所を埋めなさい。もしわからないときは、本文中から適切な単語を探して埋めましょう。

1. d _ _ _ _ _ _ = various　多様な

2. thinly, sparingly = s _ _ _ _ _ _ _　わずかに

3. b _ _ _ _ = explode, break　爆発する、勢いよく出る

4. occasional, irregular = s _ _ _ _ _ _ _　時々起こる

5. b _ _ _ _ _ = hit, pound, strike　吹きつける

6. walk, cross, navigate = t _ _ _ _ _ _ _　越える

7. s _ _ _ _ _ = move quickly and violently　高速で飛ばして行く

8. huge = c _ _ _ _ _ _ _ _　巨大な

9. p _ _ _ _ _ = lots, enough　たくさんの

10. devastating, damaging = d _ _ _ _ _ _ _ _ _ _　破壊的な

Comprehension Questions True or False

本文の内容として正しい場合は T、間違っている場合は F を書き入れなさい。

1. America experiences many different kinds of natural disasters because of geography.

2. Mt. St. Helens did very little damage to the local environment.

3. Today, there are many living things around Mt. St. Helens.

1. (　　　) 2. (　　　) 3. (　　　)

Comprehension Questions **Multiple Choice**

本文の内容について最も正しく述べているものを a～c の中から選びなさい。

1. Why were scientists monitoring Mt. St. Helens at the time of its eruption?
   a. they knew a major eruption was about to occur
   b. they wanted to catch the volcano on film
   c. they were interested in recent small eruptions

2. How did the flooding happen at the time of the eruption?
   a. glacier ice melted and flowed down the slopes
   b. a cloud of volcanic ash created a rainstorm
   c. lava cooled down in water and flowed down the slopes

3. Why is there a "word of caution" at the end of the passage?
   a. the volcano will probably erupt soon
   b. the volcano's next eruption will be more dangerous
   c. the observatory is close to the crater

Composition with Typical Expressions 🔊 Audio 15

よく使われる英語の表現を学習しましょう。日本語訳を参考に、（　　）内の単語を正しい語順に並び替えて文にしなさい。

1. 監視カメラに窃盗団が映っていた。
   (cameras, film, surveillance, on, the, thieves, caught).

_____

2. 待ち伏せしていた兵士が不意を突かれた。
   (invading, caught, the, unawares, soldiers, the, ambush).

_____

3. 注意を引かないよう静かにしていなさい。
   (quiet, attention, so, be, any, attract, don't, you).

_____

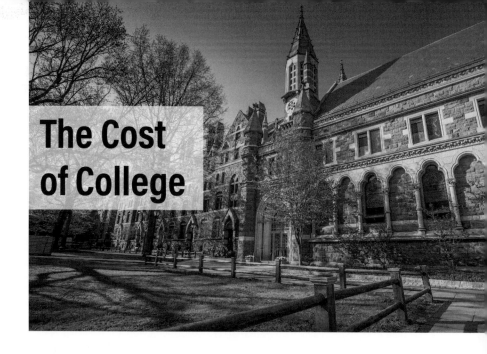

The Cost of College

米国の大学教育費は、医療費と並びここ数十年間にわたってインフレ率をはるかに上回っています。アメリカの学生は、学位取得のために莫大なローンを組んでいるのです。米国の学位はなぜこれほど魅力的で、かつ、高額な費用がかかるのでしょうか。

★ ★ ★

Pre-reading Section

Vocabulary Fill in the Blank

日本語訳をヒントに、空所に入る最も適切なものを次の中から選び、書き入れなさい。ただし、文により形を変える必要があるものが含まれています。

earnings	tuition	graduate

degree	college	undergraduate

1. 学士号は、大学の学部課程の学位である。

A bachelor's degree is an _____ degree.

2. アメリカ人は _____ も university もほとんど同じ意味の語としてよく使っている。

Americans often use the words _____ and university interchangeably.

3. 日本の大企業は昔から春に新卒者を採用している。

Large Japanese companies traditionally hire recent _____ in the spring.

4. 弁護士としての潜在的収入は大きいと私は思いますが、それが自分の望む職業かどうかわかりません。

I think the potential _____ as a lawyer are great, but I'm not sure that's the career I want.

5. 大学院の学位取得には多くの費用がかかるが、その分チャンスもある。

Earning a graduate _____ can cost a lot of money, but it can also open up opportunities.

Reading

341 words Audio 16

❶ How much is a college education worth to you? According to a 2019 OECD report, in the U.S., annual tuition averaged $8,800 at public universities and $29,500 at private institutions. In Japan, those figures were about $5,000 and $8,700, respectively.[1] But is an American education that much better? 5

❷ Tests of academic skill given to college graduates from developed countries indicate that the education is not necessarily better, as young adults who have earned a bachelor's degree from an American university tend to score below average. The real incentive is money. Typically, an undergraduate degree leads to $500,000 more in lifetime earnings. 10 There is, of course, a catch: It really depends on what you study.

❸ For example, there are thousands and thousands of graduates in exciting but highly competitive fields such as film and the arts who earn less than $50,000 a year two years after graduating, yet owe hundreds of thousands of dollars in student loans that they may never be able to pay 15 off. Who lets them borrow so unwisely?

❹ For decades, the U.S. federal government has subsidized college for Americans through a loan program that makes it very easy for students and their parents to borrow huge sums of money for tuition, fees, and living expenses. Whether or not the students pay back the loans doesn't 20 matter to universities because they get paid up front by the government.

Furthermore, after states began slashing[*2] budgets for their public universities, especially after the Great Recession[*3] of 2008-9, they were forced to find new ways of generating revenue.[*4] With guaranteed federal loans, it has been easy for public schools to keep raising tuition.

5 Meanwhile, many graduates who are saddled with enormous debt[*5] will never be able to pay off their loans. That means taxpayers will be on the hook.

❺ Unfortunately—or fortunately, depending on your point of view—international students are ineligible for these loans. Therefore, students

10 from foreign countries must find other ways to pay for the high cost of a prestigious American college education on their own. Being rich helps.

---

*1 **respectively** それぞれ
*2 **slash** 予算を削減する、切りつめる
*3 **the Great Recession** 2000年代後半〜2010年代初頭に世界市場で観察された大規模な経済的衰退の時期
*4 **generate revenue** 収益を生み出す
*5 **enormous debt** 莫大な負債

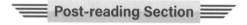

Post-reading Section

Vocabulary　Fill in the Blank

日本語訳をヒントに、空所に入る最も適切なものを次の中から選び、書き入れなさい。ただし、文により形を変える必要があるものが含まれています。

| guarantee | earn | saddle | pay off | up front | average |

1. 当社は倒産しないことを保証します。

I _____ you that our company will not go out of business.

2. ローンを組むと、家族に多額の借金を背負わせることになる。

Taking out a loan would _____ our family with too much debt.

3. このアパートに入居する前に、2ヶ月分の家賃を前払いする必要があります。

Before you move into the apartment, you'll have to pay two months' rent _____ .

4. 学位を取得しただけでは、大学卒業後すぐに就職を約束されているわけではありません。

Just _____ a degree doesn't guarantee you a job straight out of college.

5. 今年度に入ってからの月間売上は、平均して前年の2倍です。

Our monthly sales so far this year have _____ twice the amount the previous year.

Vocabulary　Synonym Practice

英英・英日の語義が成立する単語になるよう、頭文字をヒントに空所を埋めなさい。もしわからないときは、本文中から適切な単語を探して埋めましょう。

1. a _ _ _ _ _ = every year　毎年の

2. i _ _ _ _ _ _ _ = show, suggest　示す

3. i _ _ _ _ _ _ _ _ = reason, motivation　動機、駆り立てるもの

4. not allowed, can't receive = i _ _ _ _ _ _ _ _ _　資格がない、不適格な

5. r _ _ _ _ _ _ = income　収入

6. t _ _ _ _ _ _ _ _ = usually, normally　通常は

7. respectable, high-status = p _ _ _ _ _ _ _ _ _ _ _　一流の、名門の

8. costs = e _ _ _ _ _ _ _　費用

9. f _ _ _ _ _ _ _ _ _ _ = in addition, moreover　さらに

10. amount, quantity = s _ _　合計

Comprehension Questions　True or False

本文の内容として正しい場合はT、間違っている場合はFを書き入れなさい。

1. The reading passage's tone is generally critical of the American university system.

2. According to the passage, easy loans are the main cause of expensive tuition.

3. States generally increased public university budgets after the Great Recession.

1. (　　　) **2.** (　　　) **3.** (　　　)

Comprehension Questions — Multiple Choice

本文の内容について最も正しく述べているものを a 〜 c の中から選びなさい。

1. In the first paragraph, what does the word "respectively" mean?
   a. tuition is $5,000 at public universities and $8,700 at private universities in Japan
   b. tuition is $5,000 at private universities and $8,700 at public universities in Japan
   c. tuition is between $5,000 and $8,700 at public and private universities in Japan

2. According to the passage, what is the main reason to earn an expensive degree in the U.S.?
   a. it's easy to get a federal loan
   b. you will receive a better education
   c. you can probably earn more money after graduating

3. In the last paragraph, what does "or fortunately, depending on your point of view" imply?
   a. international students are lucky because they're rich
   b. international students can't get caught in the trap of easy loans and enormous debt
   c. international students don't have to pay as much for an American college education

Composition with Typical Expressions Audio 17

よく使われる英語の表現を学習しましょう。日本語訳を参考に、（　）内の単語を正しい語順に並び替えて文にしなさい。

1. 両親が亡くなって、そのカードローンの借金を私が背負うことになった。
   (credit card, died, parents, my, for their, hook, debt, the, I'm, now, and, on).

   _____

2. 家賃が安いのは、何か裏があるに違いない。
   (cheap, be, a catch, there, must, so, is, if, the, rent).

   _____

3. 利益を確保するためには、予算を削減しなければならない。
   (budget, profitable, have, slash, our, we, to, to, stay).

   _____

UNIT

9

Film

The Bar Vitelli was filmed by Francis Ford Coppola as the set of famous scenes in *The Godfather* (1972).
©Peter Turansky / Shutterstock.com

★ ★ ★

何十年もの間、ギャング映画には、日本、香港、アメリカなど、その舞台がどこであれ色あせない魅力があります。『ゴッドファーザー』は、1972 年の公開以来、数多くの映画やテレビ番組に影響を与えてきた、おそらくこのジャンルで最も影響力のある作品でしょう。

★ ★ ★

Pre-reading Section

Vocabulary Fill in the Blank

日本語訳をヒントに、空所に入る最も適切なものを次の中から選び、書き入れなさい。ただし、文により形を変える必要があるものが含まれています。

corruption   reinterpret   vulnerable

disadvantage   usher in   ruthless

1. ラグビーでは、レッドカードはチームを著しく不利な状況に追い込む。
   In rugby, a red card puts your team at a serious _____ .

2. 低平地は洪水に弱い。
   Low-lying land is _____ to flooding.

3. 父さんは情け容赦のないチェスプレイヤーで、全然勝たせてくれないんだ。
   My dad is a _____ chess player who never lets me win.

★ ★ ★

4. 多くの文明は、汚職が蔓延したあと崩壊した。

Many civilizations have collapsed after _____ became too widespread.

5. スマートフォンの発明は、デジタル技術の爆発的な革新の先駆けとなった。

The invention of the smartphone _____ an explosion of digital innovation.

Reading

❶ Who would you turn to for help if you were assaulted, robbed, or the victim[*1] of some other crime, but the police would do nothing? Would you make a deal with the mafia to exact justice? That's just what one character does in the opening scene of *The Godfather*, which was
5 released in 1972.

❷ The movie's plot[*2] concerns the affairs of the Corleone family of Italian Americans whose head, or Don, Vito Corleone, runs an organized crime group.[*3] In other words, the Corleones are in the mafia, an underground business that profits by engaging[*4] in illegal activities and exploiting
10 society's weak and vulnerable. Yet you may be surprised to learn that most viewers sympathize, to varying degrees, with Vito and his son Michael, the film's protagonist.

❸ In the movie, these men try to do what they can to protect their family and their disadvantaged Italian community to find justice in an unfair
15 world. However, they become corrupted by an American society that rewards those who are ruthless and only care about the bottom line. That story resonated with the filmgoing public at the time because of widespread disillusionment[*5] with corruption and inequality in American society. Those were the days of the unpopular Vietnam War and social
20 unrest[*6] over systemic racial discrimination.

❹ On IMDb's[*7] ranking of mafia and gangster movies, *The Godfather* ranks second, behind only *Scarface* (1983). (Al Pacino was the lead character in both.) The highest-ranking movie from the genre and older

★★★

than *The Godfather* is *Key Largo*, a 1948 film starring Classical Hollywood icon Humphrey Bogart. A study conducted in 2015 found that 81.4% of mob movies were released after *The Godfather*. Clearly, *The Godfather* ushered in a boom of mafia films. Meanwhile, its tale of a man who makes a series of poor choices to try and do what is in the interest 5 of his loved ones has been reinterpreted in numerous critically acclaimed productions, most notably two highly successful TV shows: *The Sopranos* (1999-2007) and *Breaking Bad* (2008-2013). Stories of struggle against injustice seem to have an enduring appeal.

*1 **victim** 被害者
*2 **plot** 筋書き、構想
*3 **organized crime group** 犯罪組織 (略 OCG)
*4 **engage** 関与する
*5 **disillusionment** 幻滅
*6 **social unrest** 社会不安
*7 **IMDb** Internet Movie Database。1990 年より開始し、IMDb.com 社が所有・運営する映画、テレビ番組、ストリーミング配信コンテンツなどの関連情報を集めたオンラインのデータベース。作品の概要や出演俳優のプロフィール、出演者、制作スタッフなどの作品関連情報が閲覧できる。2022 年 12 月時点でポッドキャストやテレビ放映分を含む作品は約 1,270 万点、作品や出演者に関連する画像は約 1,540 万点を収録している (公式サイト)。

Post-reading Section

Vocabulary Fill in the Blank

日本語訳をヒントに、空所に入る最も適切なものを次の中から選び、書き入れなさい。ただし、文により形を変える必要があるものが含まれています。

exploit concern varying degrees

sympathize resonate acclaimed

1. 批評家の間では人気があっても、映画を見る一般の人々の間ではそうでないことがある。

A critically _____ film may be popular among critics, but not the filmgoing public in general.

2. マーケティング担当者は、消費者の感情をどのように利用するでしょうか。

How do marketers _____ consumers' emotions?

3. この章では、ピザの起源について述べています。

This chapter _____ the origins of pizza.

4. 彼女の力強い歌詞は、絶望に苦しむ人々の心に響く。

Her powerful lyrics _____ with people suffering from depression.

5. どうして身寄りのない人を気の毒に思わずにいられるのですか？

How can you not _____ with an orphan?

Vocabulary — Synonym Practice

英英・英日の語義が成立する単語になるよう、頭文字をヒントに空所を埋めなさい。もしわからないときは、本文中から適切な単語を探して埋めましょう。

1. a _ _ _ _ _ _ = attack 暴行する、攻撃する

2. r _ _ = steal 盗む、強奪する

3. p _ _ _ _ _ _ _ _ _ = main character 主役

4. exactly = j _ _ _ まさに

5. u _ _ _ _ _ _ _ _ _ _ = hidden, illegal 隠れた、違法性のある

6. long-lasting = e _ _ _ _ _ _ _ 不朽の、長続きする

7. n _ _ _ _ _ _ = particularly, especially 特に

8. i _ _ _ _ _ _ _ _ = unfairness 不正、不当

9. allure, attraction = a _ _ _ _ _ 魅力

10. symbol, model = i _ _ _ 象徴、憧れの対象となる人

Comprehension Questions — True or False

本文の内容として正しい場合は T、間違っている場合は F を書き入れなさい。

1. In the passage, the Don of the family is its leader.

2. Injustice in the real world caused viewers to sympathize with Vito and Michael Corleone.

3. *The Godfather* is one of the most recent mob movies.

1. ( ) **2.** ( ) **3.** ( )

Comprehension Questions Multiple Choice

本文の内容について最も正しく述べているものを a～c の中から選びなさい。

1. Which answer best describes the mafia?
   a. a disorganized crime group that sells goods and services illegally
   b. an organized crime group that sells goods and services illegally
   c. an organized crime group that sells goods and services legally

2. What does it mean in the third paragraph to "only care about the bottom line"?
   a. to only care about profits
   b. to only care about family
   c. to only care about discrimination

3. Given the context of the passage, what answer is probably the best description of Classical Hollywood?
   a. an era of filmmaking that came after *The Godfather*
   b. an era of filmmaking when *The Godfather* was released
   c. an era of filmmaking that preceded *The Godfather*

Composition with Typical Expressions   Audio 19

よく使われる英語の表現を学習しましょう。日本語訳を参考に、(   ) 内の単語を正しい語順に並び替えて文にしなさい。

1. 私はいつも親友を心の支えにしています。
   (turn to, emotional, my, best friend, always, I, support, for).

   _____

2. あなたのような嘘つきと取引をするのはお断りです。
   (refuse, a liar, I, make a deal, to, with, like you).

   _____

3. 被害者は裁判を通じて正義を貫こうとした。
   (through the courts, exact justice, victim, to, sought, the).

   _____

Transgender Athletes

★★★ ―

LGBTQ の理解と取り組みは、過去数十年の間により大きな包括性 (inclusiveness) を生み出した点で進歩はあったものの、アメリカ社会で最も意見が分かれている問題の一つです。特に議論を呼んでいるのが、トランスジェンダーのアスリートが出場できる競技のルールをどう設定するかということです。彼らは男女のスポーツにどのように適合するのでしょうか?

― ★★★

Pre-reading Section

Vocabulary　Fill in the Blank

日本語訳をヒントに、空所に入る最も適切なものを次の中から選び、書き入れなさい。ただし、文により形を変える必要があるものが含まれています。

gender dysphoria　　cisgender　　critical

confer　　controversy　　hurtful

1. フィードバックが批判的すぎると、生徒はあなたの言うことを聞かなくなるかもしれませんよ。

   If your feedback is too _____ , your student might not listen to you.

2. 近年、性別違和の認知度が上がってきている。

   _____ has gained greater public recognition in recent years.

3. 私のツイッターでの不用意な発言が、これほどの論争を引き起こすとは思わなかった！

I didn't think my careless comment on Twitter would cause such a _____ !

4. 妻との口論で傷つくようなことを言うたび、私は後悔するばかりだ。

Whenever I say something _____ in an argument with my wife, I just regret it later.

5. _____ の LGBTQ への意識を高めるために、私たちにできることは何だろう。

What can we do to raise awareness of LGBTQ issues among _____ people?

Reading

335 words　Audio 20

❶ William Thomas was a man on the swim team at his college. He was a talented swimmer and did well in men's swim meets. While in college, he decided to transition into a woman because he experienced gender dysphoria, a feeling that one's gender does not match one's identity. Now a she with a new first name, Lia, the student began competing in 5 women's tournaments. As part of the gender transition, Lia took hormone therapy to suppress her testosterone levels. Reducing testosterone was also important for her swimming because the rules at the time required that she have a testosterone level consistent with the naturally occurring level in cisgender women. 10

❷ A controversy ensued when Lia began performing well at women's swimming competitions. She came close to breaking national collegiate[1] records and she won the national championship. Advocates[2] of LGBTQ rights hailed her success as a positive example for transgender women and others who do not conform to traditional ideas of gender identity 15 and roles. Detractors,[3] including current and former women's athletes, were critical because they accused Lia of retaining aspects of her male body that conferred on her an unfair advantage over competitors who were born female.

❸ In 2022, FINA, the global governing body for competitive swimming, 20 took a stand on the matter by issuing a ban on transgender women

competing in women's events if they have gone through male puberty,[4] even if they have reduced their testosterone levels, as the science on which hormones provide men with their physical advantages is not entirely clear. The rule affects not only collegiate swimming in the U.S.,
5 but also other aquatic sports like water polo and artistic swimming worldwide, even at the Olympics.

❹ Of course, the debate is hardly settled. In fact, the new rule only intensified[5] public scrutiny on the matter. Backers of FINA's rule uphold it as an example of science trumping politics, while Lia's
10 supporters assail[6] the rule as discriminatory, hurtful, and not actually based on science. Is it possible to make everyone happy?

*1 **collegiate** 大学の
*2 **advocate** 支持者、賛同する人
*3 **detractor** 中傷する人
*4 **puberty** 思春期
*5 **intensify** 激化させる
*6 **assail** 激しく非難する

=== **Post-reading Section** ===

Vocabulary \ Fill in the Blank

日本語訳をヒントに、空所に入る最も適切なものを次の中から選び、書き入れなさい。ただし、文により形を変える必要があるものが含まれています。

| transition | suppress | ensue | accuse | hail | trump |

1. ブラッドがライバル校のチームの部員を突き飛ばしたことから、グラウンドで乱闘が発生した。

A brawl _____ at the field when Brad pushed a member of a rival school's team.

2. クリーンエネルギーへの移行には多くの課題がある。

_____ to clean energy poses many challenges.

3. 私はずっと別の部屋にいたのに、なぜ私があなたのお金を盗んだと言えるのですか?!

How can you _____ me of stealing your cash when I was in another room the whole time?!

4. ジェニーはとても実利主義的です。彼女にとってお金は何より優先されます。

Jenny is so materialistic. For her, money _____ everything.

5. 黒澤明を日本の映画史上最高の監督と賞賛する人もいる。

Some _____ Akira Kurosawa as the greatest Japanese film director ever.

Vocabulary Synonym Practice

英英・英日の語義が成立する単語になるよう、頭文字をヒントに空所を埋めなさい。もしわからないときは、本文中から適切な単語を探して埋めましょう。

1. m _ _ _ = tournament, competition　大会、競技会

2. follow, accept = c _ _ _ _ _ _ 　従う

3. u _ _ _ _ _ = support, agree with　支持する

4. i _ _ _ _ _ _ _ _ = strengthen, increase　増大させる

5. keep, maintain = r _ _ _ _ _ 　保つ

6. s _ _ _ _ _ _ _ = close attention　厳格な審査

7. supporter = b _ _ _ _ _ 　支持者、支援者

8. g _ _ _ _ _ = supervise, regulate, control　管理する

9. c _ _ _ _ _ _ _ _ _ = uniform, even　一貫した

10. feature, trait = a _ _ _ _ _ 　特性

Comprehension Questions True or False

本文の内容として正しい場合は T、間違っている場合は F を書き入れなさい。

1. People with gender dysphoria feel their gender does not match their identity.

2. FINA passed a rule allowing transgender women to compete in women's swim meets.

3. There is disagreement over what science says about hormones.

1. (　　　) 2. (　　　) 3. (　　　)

★★★

Comprehension Questions Multiple Choice

本文の内容について最も正しく述べているものを a ～ c の中から選びなさい。

1. Why did Lia Thomas decide to undergo a gender transition from a man into a woman?
   - **a.** because she identifies as a man
   - **b.** because she identifies as a woman
   - **c.** because she was born with a woman's body

2. Why was there a controversy about Lia Thomas following her gender transition?
   - **a.** because she performed so poorly at women's swim meets
   - **b.** because she performed so well at men's swim meets
   - **c.** because she performed so well at women's swim meets

3. What does the author probably imply in the final sentence of the reading passage?
   - **a.** it's hard to satisfy everyone
   - **b.** it's easy to satisfy everyone
   - **c.** it's hard to debate

Composition with Typical Expressions Audio 21

よく使われる英語の表現を学習しましょう。日本語訳を参考に、(　　) 内の単語を正しい語順に並び替えて文にしなさい。

1. 今こそいじめに立ち向かうべき時だ。

   (stand, against, bullying, time, it's, take, a, to).

   _____

2. ジョージはその議論に決着をつける証拠を提示した。

   (settled, George, the, debate, that, evidence, presented).

   _____

3. オーロラは自然界に起こる素晴らしい現象です。

   (northern lights, naturally, the, phenomenon, are, occurring, an, amazing).

   _____

UNIT 11

A Poem for a President

Literature

★ ★ ★

詩はただの娯楽でしょうか、それとも人々を魅了し感動させる力を持っているのでしょうか？ 22歳の黒人女性アマンダ・ゴーマンは2021年1月、ジョー・バイデン大統領の就任式で、より良い民主主義国家をつくるための闘いを「わたしたちの登る丘」（鴻巣友季子訳、文春文庫）という詩にして朗読し、その優れた詩によって、詩が単なる娯楽ではなく人々を感動させる力を持っていることを証明しました。

—————— ★ ★ ★

Amanda Gorman attends Variety's 2021 Power of Women.
September 30, 2021. (Photo by Robyn Beck / AFP) (United States) ©AFP ／アフロ

=== **Pre-reading Section** ===

Vocabulary Fill in the Blank

日本語訳をヒントに、空所に入る最も適切なものを次の中から選び、書き入れなさい。ただし、文により形を変える必要があるものが含まれています。

| sociology | nation | activism | rioter | poetry | permanent |

1. 国家とは、国ではない。想像上のアイデンティティーである。

A _____ is not a country. It's an imagined identity.

2. 詩は4,000年以上前からある文学の一形態である。

_____ is a form of literature that dates back over 4,000 years.

3. アメリカの大学キャンパスにおける学生運動は、行き過ぎたのではないですか？

Has student _____ on American college campuses gone too far?

4. 傷は治るが、瘢痕組織^{はんこん}は永久的だ。

Wounds heal, but scar tissue is _____ .

5. 警察は催涙ガスで暴徒を散らした。

The police scattered the _____ with tear gas.

Reading

❶ Once every four years, America inaugurates a president, either a newly elected one or a president who has already served one term in office. The inauguration ceremony is a major news event, culminating with the presidential oath^{*1} of office, during which the elected president
5 swears to carry out the assigned duties.^{*2} Other elements of the inauguration include a parade, speeches, musical performances, and occasionally, a poetry reading.

❷ During the inauguration of President Joe Biden on January 21, 2021, Amanda Gorman, a 22-year-old Black woman, read her poem "The Hill
10 We Climb." It is about the long struggle of democracy to "compose a country committed to all culture, colors, characters, and conditions of man." Gorman's inspiration was the January 6th attack on the Capitol Building by supporters of former President Donald Trump who refused to accept that he had lost the election to Biden. Those rioters had sought
15 to overturn the results of the election. Gorman referenced this event with the following lines:

"We've seen a force that would shatter our nation, rather than share it. Would destroy our country if it meant delaying democracy. And this effort very nearly succeeded. But while democracy can be periodically
20 delayed, it can never be permanently defeated."^{*3}

❸ Amanda Gorman and her siblings were raised by a single mother. Gorman found solace in poetry at a young age, when she used it as a way to overcome^{*4} a speech impediment and express herself. As a teenager, she began winning major awards for her poetry. This work,

Barnes & Noble Booksellers Book Display, NYC, USA
(April, 2021) ©Alamy／アフロ

along with her activism, addresses topics such as Black identity, marginalization, feminism, and climate change. Gorman graduated from Harvard University in 2020 with a degree in sociology. The next year, she read "The Hill We Climb" at Joe Biden's inauguration. Gorman's captivating performance catapulted her to fame.*5 A few weeks later, she became the first poet to perform at the Super Bowl. She has since published works of poetry and children's literature.*6

*1 **oath** 誓い、宣誓
*2 **assigned duty** 割り当てられた任務
*3 **defeat** 負かす
*4 **overcome** 乗り越える、克服する
*5 **catapulted ~ to ...** ～が突然…の状態になる
*6 **children's literature** 児童文学

═══ **Post-reading Section** ═══

Vocabulary   Fill in the Blank

日本語訳をヒントに、空所に入る最も適切なものを次の中から選び、書き入れなさい。ただし、文により形を変える必要があるものが含まれています。

culminate   delay   inaugurate   elect   commit   marginalize

1. 本校の留学生を疎外してはいけません。
    We shouldn't _____ the foreign students at our school.

2. マジシャンのパフォーマンスは、驚くべき消失の演技で締めくくられた。
    The magician's performance _____ with an astonishing disappearing act.

3. 今年の生徒会長に選ばれるのは誰だと思う？

Who do you think will be _____ as this year's student council president?

4. 100 パーセントの覚悟が必要な重大な仕事です。

This is a serious job that requires you to be one-hundred percent _____ .

5. これ以上遅れると、私たちはプロジェクトの締切に間に合わなくなる。

If we _____ any further, we will miss the project deadline.

Vocabulary　Synonym Practice

英英・英日の語義が成立する単語になるよう、頭文字をヒントに空所を埋めなさい。もしわからないときは、本文中から適切な単語を探して埋めましょう。

1. smash, destroy = s _ _ _ _ _ _ 　壊滅させる

2. refer to, imply = r _ _ _ _ _ _ _ _ 　〜を引き合いに出す

3. s _ _ _ _ = promisc, vow 　誓う

4. a _ _ _ _ _ = admit, consent 　承諾する

5. s _ _ _ _ _ _ _ = brothers and sisters 　きょうだい

6. occasionally, sometimes = p _ _ _ _ _ _ _ _ _ _ _ 　時々

7. e _ _ _ _ _ _ = part, component 　要素

8. s _ _ _ _ _ = comfort, support 　癒し

9. o _ _ _ _ _ _ _ = reverse, cancel 　覆す

10. fascinating, enthralling = c _ _ _ _ _ _ _ _ _ _ 　人の心をつかむ

Comprehension Questions　True or False

本文の内容として正しい場合は T、間違っている場合は F を書き入れなさい。

1. A poetry reading has been part of every presidential inauguration ceremony.

2. Amanda Gorman believes that democracy always wins eventually.

3. Poetry helped Amanda Gorman overcome a speech impediment.

1. (　　　) **2.** (　　　) **3.** (　　　)

Comprehension Questions　Multiple Choice

本文の内容について最も正しく述べているものを a ～ c の中から選びなさい。

1. What is the presidential oath of office?
    a. a list of things the new president wants to do during his or her term in office
    b. a list of reasons why the new president deserves the job
    c. a promise to carry out the duties assigned to that office

2. What does "colors" mean in the phrase "all culture, colors, characters, and conditions of man"?
    a. races
    b. artistic preferences
    c. sexual orientation

3. How did Donald Trump indirectly inspire Amanda Gorman to write "The Hill We Climb"?
    a. his supporters attacked Amanda Gorman
    b. his supporters attacked the Capitol Building
    c. his supporters attacked Joe Biden

Composition with Typical Expressions　Audio 23

よく使われる英語の表現を学習しましょう。日本語訳を参考に、（　　）内の単語を正しい語順に並び替えて文にしなさい。

1. ビリー・アイリッシュは「オーシャン・アイズ」で一躍有名になった。
   (catapulted, "Ocean Eyes", song, Eilish's, to, Billie, fame, her).

_____

2. あなたの職務遂行能力のなさは受け入れられませんね。
   (your, your, duties, out, inability, carry, to, unacceptable, is).

_____

3. インディアナ・ジョーンズはジャングルで危うく殺されるところだった。
   (jungle, nearly, was, very, the, Indiana Jones, in, killed).

_____

UNIT
12

Sport

Who Were the Washington Redskins and the Cleveland Indians?

★★★

価値観は時代とともに変化します。今は良いと考えられていることばも将来は不快に感じるかもしれません。こういった傾向は、スポーツをはじめ私たちの社会や文化の至るところで見受けられます。最近アメリカの2大スポーツチームの名称が変更されましたが、新しい名称を喜んでいる人ばかりではないようなのです。

———————— ★★★

(Top) NFL - Players in the field - Washington Redskins host Atlanta Falcons at Fedex Field Stadium in Largo Maryland, on November 4, 2018. ©Jamie Lamor Thompson / Shutterstock.com (Bottom) Protesters at the Change the Mascot Rally on November 2, 2014, in Minneapolis. The protesters believe the name Washington Redskins is offensive to Native Americans. ©miker / Shutterstock.com

≡ **Pre-reading Section** ≡

Vocabulary ⟩ Fill in the Blank

日本語訳をヒントに、空所に入る最も適切なものを次の中から選び、書き入れなさい。ただし、文により形を変える必要があるものが含まれています。

| systemic | long | iconic | racial slur | investor | caricature |

1. 職場で人種的な中傷を行うことは、いかなる場合でも容認できません。

Using _____ in the workplace is unacceptable in all cases.

2. 富士山はおそらく日本を代表するシンボルです。

Mt. Fuji is perhaps the most _____ symbol of Japan.

3. 私は長い間オーストラリアに行きたいと思っていました。

I've _____ wanted to visit Australia.

4. ローマ帝国の崩壊は組織的な腐敗が原因である。

_____ corruption contributed to the collapse of the Roman Empire.

5. 株式市場が暴落したとき、投資家は大損をした。

_____ lost a ton of money when the stock market crashed.

Reading

344 words Audio 24

❶ Want to watch the Washington Redskins play football or the Cleveland Indians play baseball? Too bad. Those teams, or rather their names, don't exist anymore.

❷ The Washington Redskins began playing in the U.S. capital in 1937 when the Boston Redskins football team relocated there. The origins of 5 the football team's name, which refers to Native Americans, are not entirely clear, but it may have been inspired by a coach who introduced innovative strategies[1] from Native American football. As time passed, the meaning of "redskins" gradually became a racial slur. Pressure to change the team's name mounted,[2] but current owner Dan Snyder had 10 long refused. During America's wave of social protests over systemic racism in 2020, investors and shareholders[3] in the team's major sponsors pressured those companies to threaten to drop their financial support. This forced Snyder's hand. That year, he temporarily changed the name to the Washington Football Team. A permanent name was 15 chosen two years later: the Washington Commanders. Snyder and the head coach wanted to make a connection with the U.S. military, which has a strong presence[4] in Washington, D.C.

❸ The Cleveland Indians had a longer history, dating back to 1915. While their name was not a racial slur, its pairing with mascot Chief 20 Wahoo, a racist Native American caricature, created a problem that also grew over time, even after the Indians dropped their mascot in 2019.

After conducting surveys and interviews with the local community, the ballclub decided to become the Cleveland Guardians in 2022. The name refers to the Guardians of Traffic statues on Cleveland's Hope Memorial Bridge. They are iconic symbols of the city.

5 ❹ Reactions to the new names have been mixed. Some fans support the change as positive, while others prefer the name they had a long attachment to. Two other sports teams with names associated with[*5] Native American culture, the Kansas City Chiefs (football) and the Atlanta Braves (baseball), have also faced controversy, but the owners 10 may have less incentive to make changes due to the teams' recent successes on the field and strong fan bases.

*1 **innovative strategies** 革新的な戦略
*2 **mount** （程度が）高まる
*3 **shareholder** 株主
*4 **presence** 存在感
*5 **associate with** 〜と関連している

Post-reading Section

Vocabulary Fill in the Blank

日本語訳をヒントに、空所に入る最も適切なものを次の中から選び、書き入れなさい。ただし、文により形を変える必要があるものが含まれています。

| date | inspire | protest | conduct | threaten | pair |

1. 市民が街頭に出て政府の方針に抗議した。

Citizens took to the streets to _____ the government's policy.

2. 昨年行われた調査によると、ほとんどの消費者が当社のサービスに満足していないことがわかった。

A survey _____ last year found that most consumers are not satisfied with our service.

3. 味噌汁とピザの組み合わせは僕には邪道に思えるよ。

_____ miso soup with pizza sounds like a bad idea to me.

4. 万里の長城の最も古い部分は 2,000 年以上前にさかのぼる。

The oldest parts of the Great Wall of China _____ back to more than 2,000 years ago.

5. 私の上司は、時間通りに出勤しないなら私をクビにすると脅した。

My boss _____ to fire me if I don't start showing up to work on time.

Vocabulary Synonym Practice

英英・英日の語義が成立する単語になるよう、頭文字をヒントに空所を埋めなさい。もしわからないときは、本文中から適切な単語を探して埋めましょう。

1. m _ _ _ _ = varied　さまざまである

2. optimistic, in agreement = p _ _ _ _ _ _ _ _　肯定的な

3. p _ _ _ _ _ _ _ _ = perpetual, everlasting　永久的な

4. t _ _ _ _ _ _ _ _ _ _ = briefly, momentarily　一時的に

5. move, transfer = r _ _ _ _ _ _ _　移転する

6. love, affection = a _ _ _ _ _ _ _ _ _　愛情

7. m _ _ _ _ _ _ = built up, accumulated　積み重なった

8. r _ _ _ _ = represent, concern　関係する

9. decline, reject = r _ _ _ _ _　拒む

10. d _ _ _ _ _ _ = gave up, stopped　やめた、断念した

Comprehension Questions True or False

本文の内容として正しい場合は T、間違っている場合は F を書き入れなさい。

1. The current owner of the Washington Commanders never liked the team's old name.

2. Chief Wahoo was the mascot of the Cleveland Indians.

3. The Guardians of Traffic are statues.

1. (　　　) 2. (　　　) 3. (　　　)

Comprehension Questions Multiple Choice

本文の内容について最も正しく述べているものをa～cの中から選びなさい。

1. How much do we know about the origins of the Redskins name?
   a. they are uncertain
   b. a Native American coach chose it
   c. it was first used in Washington, D.C.

2. How did the Cleveland baseball team choose its new name, the Cleveland Guardians?
   a. a random choice
   b. a vote for the most popular name
   c. communication with the local community

3. Which of the following is true about the Kansas City Chiefs and the Atlanta Braves?
   a. they have not faced controversy
   b. they may be unlikely to change their names
   c. they have generally played poorly in recent years

Composition with Typical Expressions 🔊 Audio 25

よく使われる英語の表現を学習しましょう。日本語訳を参考に、（　　）内の単語を正しい語順に並び替えて文にしなさい。

1. 抗議運動が政府の手をわずらわせ、新しく導入された税は取り下げられた。

   (forced, the, to, tax, a, government's, drop, new, protests, hand).

   _____

2. 台風で私たちの旅程が遅れてしまい残念だ。

   (too, it's, trip, our, the, typhoon, delayed, bad).

   _____

3. コーチは彼女のフィールドでのパフォーマンスを褒めた。

   (on, her, coach, the, performance, complimented, the, field).

   _____

★ ★ ★

UNIT
13

Society

Weird Laws

★★★

外国でおかしなことが起きているという記事をオンラインで読むことはあるでしょうか。その記事は不正確だったり、より扇情的にするために話の一部を切り取っていたりするかもしれません。本章も似たようなトーンの内容です。読みながらどんな重要な情報が欠けているか想像してみてください。

★★★

Pre-reading Section

Vocabulary Fill in the Blank

日本語訳をヒントに、空所に入る最も適切なものを次の中から選び、書き入れなさい。ただし、文により形を変える必要があるものが含まれています。

better   hardcore   criminal   exception   matter   charge

1. 今年もサンタクロースからプレゼントが欲しかったら、いい子にしていなさいね。

   You _____ be a good little girl if you want presents from Santa Claus this year.

2. このような罪状によって、あなたは長期にわたり刑務所に入ることになるかもしれません。

   These _____ against you could put you in prison for a long time.

3. 残念ながら、その航空会社のキャンセルポリシーには、病気の子供に対する例外規定があありません。

Unfortunately, the airline's cancellation policy doesn't have an _____ for sick kids.

4. 何度誘われても、あなたとはデートに行きません！

I am not going on a date with you, no _____ how many times you ask!

5. このビデオゲームの激しさは、私にはちょっと露骨すぎます。

The violence in this video game is a bit too _____ for me.

Reading

350 words 🔊 Audio 26

❶ Are you planning a trip to the U.S.? Better know your state laws! Each of America's 50 states has some unusual rules that could put you on the wrong side of the law.

❷ Have you ever sat outside a convenience store with a friend to have a
5 snack or drink? Leave that attitude at home if you're in Reno, Nevada! Lots of things are legal in Nevada, including gambling and prostitution, but sitting on the sidewalk in downtown Reno is certainly not one of them. Not even if you bring your own chair! But there are exceptions, including medical emergencies, wheelchair users, watching a parade,
10 and waiting for a bus.

❸ If you find yourself in North Carolina instead of Nevada but you still want some gaming excitement, you could play bingo. But until a few years ago, you could forget about consuming alcohol, no matter what your age! Although bingo is a simple game you can probably play
15 correctly after a beer or two, selling or consuming alcohol in a bingo parlor was illegal in North Carolina until 2019.

❹ Speaking of games and the Carolinas, nobody under the age of 18 can legally play a pinball machine in South Carolina. Better bring your ID if you want some extreme pinball excitement here! (Actually, nobody
20 enforces this law. Which begs the question: Why does it exist?)

★★★

❺ If pinball isn't dangerous enough for you, head to New Jersey. The criminals there are so hardcore, the state had to take serious action. Now it is a crime to wear body armor in New Jersey...while committing another crime. That's right! If you don't want to face two criminal charges, leave that bulletproof vest at home next time you rob a bank. 5

❻ But maybe you're looking for a more peaceful state. How about Oregon? If you're in a cemetery, you don't have to worry about a hunter accidentally shooting you. Why? Because hunting in cemeteries is illegal! Of course, you could be shot by a hunter who's ignorant of or blatantly ignoring the law. Still, having the law on the books is better than 10 nothing!

≣ **Post-reading Section** ≣

Vocabulary Fill in the Blank

日本語訳をヒントに、空所に入る最も適切なものを次の中から選び、書き入れなさい。ただし、文により形を変える必要があるものが含まれています。

| beg | speaking | consume | rob | ignore | enforce |

1. 食事と言えば、お昼ごはんはどこで食べたいですか？

_____ of food, where do you want to have lunch?

2. 警察官の仕事は、法律を行使することです。

A police officer's job is to _____ the law.

3. 彼のヨーロッパ旅行は、強盗に遭ったとき台無しになった。

His trip to Europe was ruined when he got _____ .

4. 私が話しているときに無視しないでよ！

Don't _____ me when I'm talking to you!

5. ジャンクフードの摂り過ぎは、深刻な健康問題を引き起こす可能性がある。

_____ too much junk food can lead to serious health problems.

Vocabulary — Synonym Practice

英英・英日の語義が成立する単語になるよう、頭文字をヒントに空所を埋めなさい。もしわからないときは、本文中から適切な単語を探して埋めましょう。

1. e _ _ _ _ = to be　存在する

2. h _ _ _ = go　行く

3. against the law, not legal = i _ _ _ _ _ _ _　違法な

4. i _ _ _ _ _ _ _ _ = clueless, not knowing　愚かな、無知な

5. a _ _ _ _ _ _ _ _ _ _ _ = not on purpose　うっかり

6. do = c _ _ _ _ _　実行する

7. graveyard = c _ _ _ _ _ _ _ _　墓地

8. b _ _ _ _ _ _ _ _ = obviously, purposely　あからさまに

9. illegal act = c _ _ _ _　犯罪、違法行為

10. p _ _ _ _ _ _ _ = safe, calm　落ち着いた

Comprehension Questions — True or False

本文の内容として正しい場合は T、間違っている場合は F を書き入れなさい。

1. It is currently illegal to drink alcohol in a bingo parlor in North Carolina.

2. In New Jersey, wearing body armor and robbing a bank are two separate crimes.

3. The Carolinas are North Carolina and South Carolina.

1. (　　　) 2. (　　　) 3. (　　　)

Comprehension Questions Multiple Choice

本文の内容について最も正しく述べているものを a ～ c の中から選びなさい。

1. Why does the passage imply that the law in Reno is silly?
   a. because you have to bring your own chair
   b. because gambling and prostitution are legal in Nevada
   c. because you have to stand while waiting for the bus

2. Why does the South Carolina law about the legal age to play pinball exist?
   a. to make pinball more exciting
   b. nobody enforces this law
   c. the passage doesn't tell us why

3. Why does the passage suggest that Oregon is safer than New Jersey?
   a. because hunting in cemeteries is illegal in Oregon
   b. because hunting in cemeteries is illegal in New Jersey
   c. because hunting in cemeteries is legal in New Jersey

Composition with Typical Expressions 🔊 Audio 27

よく使われる英語の表現を学習しましょう。日本語訳を参考に、（　　）内の単語を正しい語順に並び替えて文にしなさい。

1. アル・カポネは、生涯の大半を違法行為をして過ごしていた。

   (his life, was, on the wrong, Al Capone, most of, side, of the law).

   _____

2. そんな態度はやめなさい。さもないと学校で困ることになりますよ。

   (that, at, attitude, school, trouble, get in, leave, home, or, you'll, at).

   _____

3. 私たちは、有効だがとても古い法律を改定する必要がある。

   (the books, we, very, laws, should, old, some, on, update).

   _____

UNIT 14

Work

Careers in Crisis

★★★
1990 年代初頭のバブル経済崩壊後、日本は「失われた 10 年」と呼ばれる長期的な経済不況に陥りました。この時代に社会人となった多くの成人は、彼らの親世代よりもキャリアを築く機会が少なかったのです。2008 年から 2009 年にかけてのアメリカの大不況も、ミレニアル世代に同じような影響を及ぼしています。
★★★

=== **Pre-reading Section** ===

Vocabulary　Fill in the Blank

日本語訳をヒントに、空所に入る最も適切なものを次の中から選び、書き入れなさい。ただし、文により形を変える必要があるものが含まれています。

sanguine	impression	common threat
dogged	image	rainy-day fund

1. 緊急時に使うための資金を準備しておくべきだ。

You should prepare a _____ to use in emergencies.

2. あなたは私の服装が好きじゃないみたいね。

I have the _____ that you don't like my outfit.

3. もっと素敵な服装であれば、より良い印象を与えると思いますよ。

If you dressed nicer, I think you'd have a better _____ .

4. あなたは暗号通貨ビジネスへの期待が大きすぎるかもしれません。

Your expectations about your cryptocurrency business may be too _____ .

5. ひたすら真実を追い求めた結果、彼女はついに実の両親の身元がわかった。

After a _____ pursuit of the truth, she finally learned the identity of her biological parents.

Reading

347 words   Audio 28

❶ "If you put your mind to it, you can accomplish[*1] anything." This famous quote from the 1985 movie *Back to the Future* is a perfect example of the boundless optimism Americans are known for. It's an attitude that has driven entrepreneurs[*2] to take risks, artists to doggedly pursue[*3] dreams, and college students to let passion guide their choice of 5 major.

❷ For young adults embarking on careers in 2008 and 2009, the Great Recession turned those sanguine expectations on their head. As stock markets crashed, home values plummeted, and workers lost jobs on a scale not seen in America since the Great Depression[*4] of the 1930s, job 10 opportunities disappeared and career plans went up in smoke for millennials, the generation born between 1981 and 1996. The long-term economic impact for these young Americans is that they tend to have lower incomes, fewer assets, and more debt than previous generations did at their age. Some consider them a "lost generation" that has delayed 15 milestones such as marriage, having children, and buying a home. In the 2010s, meanwhile, the spread of social media, which incentivizes users to present the best image of themselves, fueled millennials' anxiety. The impression they received was that "everyone's happy except me."

❸ Today, a notable number of millennials live life exercising either great 20 caution or adopting a carefree, you-only-live-once attitude. The former

★★★

may do more to prepare rainy-day funds, while the latter may hop between low-paying but flexible jobs that allow them to enjoy travel and new experiences. One common thread, however, is that millennials have a greater mistrust of financial institutions[*5] than prior generations.

5 ❹ Their fears may have been justified. Just over a decade later, the COVID-19 pandemic upended this generation's lives again. The dramatic economic downturn and precipitous drop[*6] in employment amid lockdowns that failed to halt the spread of the SARS-CoV-2 virus seemed to confirm millennials' misgivings about finance and capitalism. In the wake of the
10 pandemic, turbulent stock markets, inflation, and concerns about war disrupting the international order are among the shocks unsettling their careers and long-term plans for a second time.

---

*1 **accomplish** 達成する
*2 **entrepreneur** 起業家
*3 **pursue** 追い求める
*4 **the Great Depression** 世界大恐慌 (1929 年 9 月に米国株価の大暴落から始まり世界に広がった経済不況)
*5 **institution** 機関、機関投資家
*6 **precipitous drop** 急落

═══ Post-reading Section ═══

Vocabulary **Fill in the Blank**

日本語訳をヒントに、空所に入る最も適切なものを次の中から選び、書き入れなさい。ただし、文により形を変える必要があるものが含まれています。

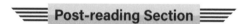

crash   justify   hop   plummet   present   halt

1. あの人に気をつけて。彼は常に女友達の間を行き来しているから。
Look out for that guy. He's constantly _____ between girlfriends.

2. 私は崖の端につまずき、海へ真っ逆さまに落ちてしまった。
I tripped over the edge of the cliff and _____ into the ocean.

3. あなたは嫌かもしれないけど、人はあなたの見せ方次第であなたを判断します。

You may not like it, but people judge you depending on how you _____ yourself.

4. 原子力発電所の運転を停止した場合、私たちは失われた電力をどう補うのでしょう。

If we _____ nuclear power plant operations, how will we replace the lost power?

5. どうしていじめを正当化できるのですか?!

How can you possibly _____ bullying?!

Vocabulary　Synonym Practice

英英・英日の語義が成立する単語になるよう、頭文字をヒントに空所を埋めなさい。もしわからないときは、本文中から適切な単語を探して埋めましょう。

1. p _ _ _ _ = previous　前の

2. m _ _ _ _ _ _ _ _ = important event, highlight　記念すべき出来事、節目

3. a _ _ _ = during, in the middle of　渦中の

4. concern, unease = a _ _ _ _ _ _　心配、不安

5. t _ _ _ _ _ _ _ _ = wild, unstable　不安定な、乱れた

6. b _ _ _ _ _ _ _ _ = unlimited, endless　果てしない

7. period of ten years = d _ _ _ _ _　10年間

8. m _ _ _ _ = specialty, area of expertise　専攻

9. e _ _ _ _ _ _ _ = practice, use　実践する

10. start or begin a journey or phase = e _ _ _ _ _ _　乗り出す、始める

Comprehension Questions　True or False

本文の内容として正しい場合はT、間違っている場合はFを書き入れなさい。

1. The Great Recession made millennials more optimistic.

2. Millennials place less trust in financial institutions than previous generations.

3. COVID-19 confirmed millennials' fears of another economic crisis.

1. (　　　) 2. (　　　) 3. (　　　)

Comprehension Questions Multiple Choice

本文の内容について最も正しく述べているものを a 〜 c の中から選びなさい。

1. What phrase best describes a "lost generation"?
   a. a generation with fewer career opportunities and wealth
   b. a generation with more career opportunities and wealth
   c. a generation with fewer career opportunities and more wealth

2. According to the passage, what is one downside of social media?
   a. social media encourages a carefree, you-only-live-once attitude
   b. social media is a bad way to shape your image
   c. social media can give you the impression that everybody else is happier than you

3. What does the passage's author probably think about the quote from *Back to the Future*?
   a. it is too famous
   b. it is too optimistic
   c. it is too realistic

Composition with Typical Expressions 🔊 Audio 29

よく使われる英語の表現を学習しましょう。日本語訳を参考に、（   ）内の単語を正しい語順に並び替えて文にしなさい。

1. 量子力学は、私たちの宇宙に対する理解を覆すかもしれません。
   (turn, understanding of, the universe, quantum mechanics, may, on its head, our).

   _____

2. ウクライナに留学する予定が戦争によって駄目になった。
   (plans, went up, because of, the war, my, Ukraine, in smoke, to study, in).

   _____

3. 人生一度きりなので、リスクを取ることにした。
   (only, decided, take, I, risk, you, once, because, live, a, to).

   _____

UNIT
15

Politics

What Is *Roe v. Wade?*

JUSTICE HAS NOT CHANGED SINCE 1973

Women's March in Washington demanding continued access to abortion after the ban on most abortions in Texas, and looming threat to *Roe v. Wade* in upcoming Supreme Court. ©Peter Turansky / Shutterstock.com

★ ★ ★

どの国の政治にも大論争となる問題があります。政治を巡り対立が激化しているアメリカには、こうした問題が数多くあります。中でも一番大きな問題は中絶でしょう。最近、合衆国最高裁判所での判決が議論の中心になっていますが、その中絶の可否について大きな変化がありました。

★ ★ ★

Pre-reading Section

Vocabulary ▶ Fill in the Blank

日本語訳をヒントに、空所に入る最も適切なものを次の中から選び、書き入れなさい。ただし、文により形を変える必要があるものが含まれています。

contraception   mortality   former

latter   regardless   first-hand

1. 竜巻が近所を襲ったとき、私はその破壊力を直に体験した。

I witnessed a tornado's destruction _____ when one ripped through my neighborhood.

2. 日本では出産時の乳幼児死亡率が驚くほど低い。

Infant _____ during childbirth is incredibly low in Japan.

★ ★ ★

3. 生きるか死ぬかの選択なら、ほとんどの人は前者を取るだろう。

If it's a choice between living and dying, most people would take the _____ .

4. 彼の妻は信仰上の理由により避妊をしません。

His wife doesn't use _____ because of her religious beliefs.

5. 仕事に遅れると、理由に関係なくその日の給料が減額されます。

If you're late to work, your pay for the day will be reduced, _____ of the reason.

Reading

❶ Considering an abortion is a dreadful predicament nobody wants, though some women unfortunately find themselves in it. But even if an American woman decides to get an abortion, it has not always been available. Before 1973, each state set its own laws regulating[*1] the
5 procedure. In New York in the early 1900s, for example, there were legal barriers to abortion and even sharing information about contraception. Poor, uneducated Americans experienced higher rates of infant and maternal[*2] mortality and deaths from botched illegal abortions. Margaret Sanger, a nurse, witnessed these horrible circumstances first-
10 hand. She devoted her life to giving women access to birth control. Gradually, public opinion shifted in favor of greater access to contraception and, to a lesser degree, abortions. Then came *Roe v. Wade*.

❷ This 1973 Supreme Court case set a national guideline for abortion. The plaintiff,[*3] whose name, Jane Roe, was an alias to protect her
15 identity, was a Texas woman who sued Henry Wade, the district attorney of Dallas County, where abortion was illegal. As a compromise,[*4] the court ruled that a woman has the right to an abortion through the first trimester[*5] and that a state may regulate access from then.

❸ After *Roe v. Wade*, abortion became an increasingly hot-button issue[*6]
20 in American politics, pitting the pro-life side (those opposed to abortion) against pro-choice supporters (those pushing for legal abortions). A typical argument among the former is that abortion is murder, while the latter say women should have control of their bodies.

★★★

❹ The two major political parties[*7] have squared off[*8] over the issue. Americans who are more religious tend to be pro-life and support the Republican Party,[*9] while the Democratic Party's[*10] supporters are generally pro-choice. A Supreme Court[*11] nominee's stance on abortion has become a "litmus test" for many politicians that determines their 5 support, regardless of other factors. In recent years, the Supreme Court's nine members have become mostly nominees of Republican presidents, and in 2022, their ruling in the case *Dobbs v. Jackson Women's Health Organization* overturned *Roe v. Wade.* Now, each state sets its own abortion laws again. 10

*1　**regulate** 規制する、制限する　　*2　**maternal** 母親の、母方の
*3　**plaintiff** 原告　　　　　　　　*4　**compromise** 和解
*5　**first trimester** 妊娠初期の３ヶ月間 (米国では臨月を９ヶ月目とし、妊娠９ヶ月を３分割して first
　　trimester → second trimester → third[last] trimester としている。)
*6　**hot-button issue** 激しい議論を巻き起こす問題
*7　**political party** 政党
*8　**square off** にらみ合う、対決する
*9　**Republican Party** 共和党 (1854~)
*10 **Democratic Party** 民主党 (1828~)
*11 **Supreme Court** 合衆国最高裁判所 (the Supreme Court of the Unites States、首都ワシントン D.C. にある。)

═ **Post-reading Section** ═

Vocabulary　**Fill in the Blank**

日本語訳をヒントに、空所に入る最も適切なものを次の中から選び、書き入れなさい。ただし、文により形を変える必要があるものが含まれています。

rule　　sue　　pit　　overturn　　devote　　botch

1. パートナーが実験に失敗したため、私たちは科学プロジェクトを完了することができませんでした。

We couldn't complete the science project because my partner _____ the lab experiment.

2. 今年のワールドシリーズは、セントルイス・カージナルスとボストン・レッドソックスの対戦です。

This year's World Series _____ the St. Louis Cardinals against the Boston Red Sox.

3. 裁判所は、会社が事故の影響を受けた住民に補償しなければならない、と判決を下した。

The court has _____ that the company must compensate residents affected by the accident.

4. 彼女は、障害を持って生まれた子供たちを助けるために、医師としてのキャリアを捧げるつもりだ。

She plans to _____ her career as a doctor to helping children born with disabilities.

5. 最高裁判所が下級審の有罪判決を覆せば、彼は収監を免れることができる。

He can avoid prison if the Supreme Court _____ the lower court's guilty verdict.

Vocabulary — Synonym Practice

英英・英日の語義が成立する単語になるよう、頭文字をヒントに空所を埋めなさい。もしわからないときは、本文中から適切な単語を探して埋めましょう。

1. d _ _ _ _ _ _ _ = horrible, terrible, awful　ひどい、恐ろしい

2. baby = i _ _ _ _ _　乳児

3. o _ _ _ _ _ _ = against　反対した

4. see, watch = w _ _ _ _ _ _　目の当たりにする、立ち会う

5. c _ _ _ _ _ _ _ _ _ _ _ _ = situation　事情、状況

6. s _ _ _ _ _ = position, view, opinion　立場

7. candidate = n _ _ _ _ _ _　候補者

8. operation, surgery = p _ _ _ _ _ _　手術

9. r _ _ _ _ _ = decision, verdict, judgement　決定、判決

10. problem, dilemma = p _ _ _ _ _ _ _ _ _　困難、苦しい状況

Comprehension Questions — True or False

本文の内容として正しい場合は T、間違っている場合は F を書き入れなさい。

1. Abortion was completely illegal in the U.S. before 1973.

2. Margaret Sanger worked hard to increase women's access to birth control.

3. Today, different states have different laws about abortion.

1. (　　) 2. (　　) 3. (　　)

★★★

Comprehension Questions \ Multiple Choice

本文の内容について最も正しく述べているものを a〜c の中から選びなさい。

1. What was the result of *Roe v. Wade*?
   a. women were given the right to an abortion at anytime
   b. women were given the right to an abortion after the first trimester of pregnancy ended
   c. women were given the right to an abortion through the first trimester of pregnancy

2. What does the passage imply about the connection between religion and views on abortion?
   a. stronger religiosity correlates with pro-life views
   b. stronger religiosity correlates with pro-choice views
   c. weaker religiosity correlates with pro-life views

3. What is a major reason, according to the passage, why *Roe v. Wade* was overturned?
   a. most of the Supreme Court's current members were Democratic nominees
   b. most of the Supreme Court's current members were Republican nominees
   c. most of the Supreme Court's current members are religious

Composition with Typical Expressions \ 🔊 Audio 31

よく使われる英語の表現を学習しましょう。日本語訳を参考に、(　　) 内の単語を正しい語順に並び替えて文にしなさい。

1. なぜ日本では中絶が話題にならないのですか。

   (isn't, Japan, abortion, hot-button, why, issue, a, in)?

   _____

2. 困っているときに助けてくれるかどうかで、その人が友達だと判断する基準になる。

   (litmus test, I'm in, for friends, my, is, they, me, if, when, trouble, help).

   _____

3. 森で猟師が熊と対決した。

   (squared, woods, a, in, against, bear, the, hunter, off, a).

   _____

About the Author

Alexander Farrell（アレクサンダー・ファレル）

米国テキサス大学オースティン校歴史学科卒業、サルヴェ・レジーナ大学大学院国際関係学科修了。2003年より京都市在住。日英翻訳者として、日本政府観光局をはじめ、ノンフィクション作品・書籍、ニュース・雑誌記事、広告、企業プレスリリース等に数多く携わる。関西地方を中心に全国の観光地の旅行記事を作成し、トラベルライターとして現地取材も行なっているほか、Alamy、Getty Images でトラベルフォトグラファーとしても活動している。英語教科書に *Creative Ideas for Products & Services*『商品開発の現場から ── アイデア・人・モノの融合』（訳、松柏社）、*America Today*『米国の今：文化・社会・歴史』（松柏社）。

Official website ▶ www.kyotoandbeyond.com

📷 Cover photos 🖼

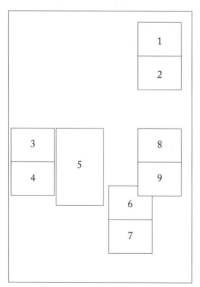

America's Evolution
今のアメリカ、これからのアメリカ

2023 年 4 月 10 日　初版第 1 刷発行

著　　者　Alexander Farrell

発 行 者　森　信久
発 行 所　**株式会社　松 柏 社**
　　　　　〒102－0072　東京都千代田区飯田橋 1－6－1
　　　　　TEL　03 (3230) 4813（代表）
　　　　　FAX　03 (3230) 4857
　　　　　http://www.shohakusha.com
　　　　　e-mail: info@shohakusha.com

装　　幀　小島トシノブ（NONdesign）
組　　版　木野内宏行（ALIUS）
印刷・製本　シナノ書籍印刷株式会社
ISBN978-4-88198-783-4
略　　号 ＝ 783
Copyright © 2023 Alexander Farrell